Elizabeth Bishop: A Very Short Introduction

VERY SHORT INTRODUCTIONS are for anyone wanting a stimulating and accessible way into a new subject. They are written by experts, and have been translated into more than 45 different languages.

The series began in 1995, and now covers a wide variety of topics in every discipline. The VSI library currently contains over 700 volumes—a Very Short Introduction to everything from Psychology and Philosophy of Science to American History and Relativity—and continues to grow in every subject area.

Very Short Introductions available now:

Available soon:

For more information visit our website

www.oup.com/vsi/

Jonathan F. S. Post

ELIZABETH
BISHOP

A Very Short Introduction

OXFORD
UNIVERSITY PRESS

Great Clarendon Street, Oxford, OX2 6DP,
United Kingdom

Oxford University Press is a department of the University of Oxford.
It furthers the University's objective of excellence in research, scholarship,
and education by publishing worldwide. Oxford is a registered trade mark of
Oxford University Press in the UK and in certain other countries

First edition published in 2022

Impression: 1

Published in the United States of America by Oxford University Press
198 Madison Avenue, New York, NY 10016, United States of America

British Library Cataloguing in Publication Data
Data available

Library of Congress Control Number: 2021947772

ISBN 978-0-19-885141-7

Printed in Great Britain by
Ashford Colour Press Ltd, Gosport, Hampshire

For Susan, Jessica, and Fred
'—the dark ajar, the rocks breaking with light'.

Contents

Acknowledgements

I owe a collective note of thanks to the many hands who helped with the creation of *Elizabeth Bishop: A Very Short Introduction*. To the group of salty readers by the sea in Stonington Connecticut, for whom Elizabeth Bishop's poetry formed a compass rose for bi-weekly readings in the long, pre-pandemic summer of 2019: Kenneth Bleeth, Jeff Callahan, Lynn Callahan, Susan Gallick, Belinda de Kay, Tertius de Kay, David Laurence, David Leeming, Pam Leeming, James Longenbach, Sibby Lynch, Laura Mathews, Julie Rivkin, Joanna Scott, Willard Spiegelman, and Stuart Vyse. To Chelsea Mitchell, Director of the Woolworth Library of the Stonington Historical Center, and Nan Danforth, for help gathering two rarely seen photos of Bishop by Rollie McKenna. And to Belinda de Kay, Gregory Dowling, Susan Gallick, and Stephen Yenser for reading early chapters with care and offering suggestions and encouragement.

No one could wish for a better, more generous trio of readers of the whole manuscript than Langdon Hammer, James Longenbach, and Mary Jo Salter. This book would be the poorer without the special gifts they bring to the study of Elizabeth Bishop. I am grateful as well to Curtis Whitaker for finishing touches supplied to the final draft. During the pandemic, when this book was in production, Jenny Nugee at Oxford University Press proved again to be the ablest of editors. Although this is not a scholarly tome, I hope it conveys something of what I've learned from the great variety of Bishop readers who now populate the world. Finally, a note of remembrance to Joseph and U. T. Summers, and to my mother, Margaret Post, who many years ago made Bishop into a household word. This book is dedicated to my wife and our two children.

List of illustrations

'Yes, all my life I have lived and behaved very much like that sandpiper [in her poem, "Sandpiper"]—just running along the edges of different countries and continents, "looking for something". I have always felt I couldn't *possibly* live very far inland, away from the ocean; and I *have* always lived near it, frequently in sight of it. Naturally I know, and it has been pointed out to me, that most of my poems are geographical, or about coasts, beaches and rivers running to the sea, and most of the titles of my books are geographical too.'

—Elizabeth Bishop, 1976, accepting the Neustadt
International Prize for Literature.

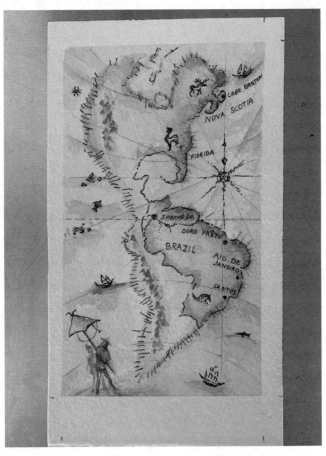

1. Map, after the 1658 Visscher Map of North and South America.

Chapter 1
Less is more: a world in miniature

The Bishop phenomenon

'Dear Millicent: I think this wd have been a better photograph if the photographer hadn't been so careful to get the sun, or moon, exactly on the top of the mast' (Figure 2). The remark, like so many by Elizabeth Bishop, says much in little. It is written on a postcard, one instance in a voluminous correspondence that kept her connected to a larger world during a lifetime of travel. It forms

2. B. A. King, *Lobster Boat* (1977).

an observation, in this case, of a small seascape with a lobster boat. (Bishop always preferred small to large, shoreline to inland.) And it is exact in stating a preference, a matter of taste, for the in-exact, the off-balance, the imperfect, the line that isn't straight, the seemingly inessential. It even leaves room for error—on her part. Is it an image of the sun or moon on top of that mast? She pauses. She isn't sure. Modesty and boldness seem part of a single mind. 'I think'.

In what turned out to be the final year of her life, Bishop sent this postcard to her friend Millicent Pettit, whose house on the island of North Haven, off the coast of Maine, Bishop occasionally rented with her partner Alice Methfessel. Bishop died on 6 October 1979 of a cerebral aneurysm in her wharf-side condominium on Boston Harbor. By then she was a much-admired poet but not as celebrated as she would become in the years following her death. Where many poets' reputations decline after death, hers has been constantly on the rise, climbing, it seems, with each decade, and in the process spreading beyond the USA and Canada to England, Scotland, Wales, and Ireland, with a distant reach south to Brazil and Australia.

Who is this person, this poet? Born in 1911, Bishop came of age as a poet in mid-century, perhaps best symbolized by her appointment as Poetry Consultant for the Library of Congress for 1949–50; and it is fair to say that many now regard her as the finest lyric poet (certainly the 'most beloved') in the English-speaking world of the second half of the 20th century. True, the names of W. B. Yeats, T. S. Eliot, Ezra Pound, Robert Frost, and William Carlos Williams, lofty modernists from the first half of the 20th century, might be more familiar to the general reader, attached as they often are to a national or international identity. Bishop's name and fortunes ride a different wave. More tied to geographical region than to country, she appeals to readers who identify with the quotidian and the human (but not at the expense of the natural world), rather than with the political state; with the particulars of home and the home-made rather than the concept of homeland or an overarching poetics. 'I like the way her whole *oeuvre* is on the scale of a human life,' writes the American poet James Merrill; 'there is no oracular amplification, she doesn't go about on stilts to make her vision wider.'

'Her whole *oeuvre*' represents an astonishingly small number of published poems—about 90 in all. The majority are found in the four individual volumes of verse that Bishop saw into print and serve as the primary focus of this *Very Short Introduction*: *North & South* (1946), *A Cold Spring* (1955), *Questions of Travel* (1965), and *Geography III* (1976). Another 10 or so poems appear in her several volumes of *New and Collected Poems* (1969, 1983), each volume rather confusingly called at the time *The Complete Poems*. These volumes also include a few translations and some juvenilia. If you're counting, as I am for the moment, her productivity comes down to about a volume of poems a decade for the years she was active as a poet, or, on average, about two poems published a year. Her last volume, *Geography III*, is a mere 10 poems. To make a book out of them, the publishers had to widen the margins.

No 20th-century poet has gone so far with so little, has made such a virtue out of scarcity. Contributing to the seeming smallness of the corpus, too, is the absence of prolegomenon, preface, or apologia about poetics. Not that Bishop didn't have firm ideas about art, almost from the beginning, but in contrast to all the poets named above, she hardly ever opined in public on the matter. When she wrote prose—and Bishop wrote lucid, lively prose—it assumed, instead, the form of short stories, especially early on in life; the occasional brief essay or memoir; the rare blurb for another poet; or the vignette, 'Sub-Tropics', as she called them on one occasion, on toads, crabs, and snails. Nothing, in short, that might be considered self-promotional. About the only kind of writing to which one might attach the word 'vast' or 'voluminous' is her private correspondence with others, and vast and voluminous it certainly is.

Preciousness not being an evitable consequence of scarcity, how is it that Bishop made her way to the top? Initially, she was regarded as a poet's poet, although even here the familiar honorific is special. Those who first praised and supported her were themselves unusual in their merit and visibility. They constitute almost a 'who's who' of 20th-century poets bordering both sides of the Atlantic. Her modernist mentor in the 1930s and 1940s, Marianne Moore, was a crucial first reader, whom a shy but enterprising Bishop sought out while still a college student. Then came Robert Lowell and Randall Jarrell in the 1940s, as admiring peers and reviewers, followed by the slightly younger John Ashbery and James Merrill in the 1960s and 1970s, and many more poets after that, including a hospitable Seamus Heaney, an initially repelled Adrienne Rich, and a host of 'New Generation Poets' from England in the 1990s, right up to the present day. In retrospect, it would be hard to imagine a more substantial pedigree or lineage.

How the notoriously reticent Bishop earned the attention and respect of her peers, their loyalty, friendship, and support, is a fascinating story, as the biographies remind us. The support of others depended, in part, not just on the perceived originality of her verse and her likeable presence but on her epistolary talents for initiating and sustaining friendship through the exchange of advice and affection. (Bishop is one of the great letter writers of her century.) The ensuing friendships inspired more than a few memorable phrases that capture important qualities of her verse that have become part of the Bishop legend. Here is the final line from one of Lowell's four sonnets to Bishop: 'unerring Muse who makes the casual perfect'. A near 'perfect' description of a chief feature of Bishop's verse (only near perfect because Bishop would never think of herself as an 'unerring Muse'), it points to the significant shaping of everyday speech in her verse. Bishop can attach a simple word like 'yes', overheard on a late afternoon bus travelling westward, to a line of thought stitched together by perhaps the oldest rhyme in English, with the answering term (death) serving as the proper close, as evening turns into night:

> 'Yes'…that peculiar
> affirmative. 'Yes…'
> A sharp, indrawn breath,
> half groan, half acceptance,
> that means 'Life's like that.
> We know *it* (also death).'

Casual speech, readily accessible, but filled with understanding about how the world turns.

From a different angle, here is an admiring Merrill (again): 'Among topheavy wrecks, she stays afloat,' he notes in a brief poem of his own called 'Her Craft'. Merrill's pun in the title captures at once Bishop's preferred means of slow travel by boat and the corresponding long attention she gave to her art, her craft. (Her slowness composing poems is legendary, as is her guilt over not writing enough.) The quoted line also suggests an aesthetics of survival, the lightness of 'less is more', as Merrill hints at the overreaching that made wrecks of so many of her generation, including, at times, Lowell.

And now Heaney, writing much later about shifting fashions and the elevation of Bishop over the most famous of mid-century poets in the USA, Robert Lowell:

> Lowell is taking the punishment that's always handed out to the big guy eventually; so no, I'm not surprised. Lowell was a white Anglo-Saxon Protestant male, a Eurocentric, egotistical sublime, writing as if he intended to be heard in a high wind. He was on the winning side from the start: Boston Brahmin, friend of Eliot, part of the literary establishment on both sides of the Atlantic—although he was, of course, ever-conscious about these advantages, and

forever making his courtly bows, in public and in private, to Elizabeth and her achievement. But then the fashion shifted, the culture favored a less imperious style, the gender balance needed adjusting, the age of Merrill and Ashbery arrived, chamber music and cabaret rather than orchestral crash were in favor, and the time was propitious for the perfect pitch of Bishop.

Yes, Bishop's 'perfect pitch'. An example, drawn again from 'The Moose':

> Goodbye to the elms,
> to the farm, to the dog.
> The bus starts. The light
> grows richer; the fog,
> shifting, salty, thin,
> comes closing in.

The carefully marked pauses, the simple rhyme of 'dog' with 'fog', allow each word or phrase its distinct note, with the final rhyme bringing this description to a lightly quickened evening close.

Other factors of a more serendipitous and scholarly order have contributed to her elevation. As Heaney's commentary suggests, Bishop's emergence as a poet coincided with the widespread admission of women into the academy in the late 1960s and 1970s, at both the undergraduate and graduate levels. Although women had long taken courses at Harvard, for instance, the university only became officially coeducational in the years immediately prior to Bishop's teaching there in the early 1970s in what would be her only continuous stretch of employment. Until then, Bishop had supported herself mainly through a combination of fellowships, a small trust fund, earnings from her writings, a brief stint at teaching at the University of Washington, and the hospitality of friends. In the case of her stay with her Brazilian lover, the politically prominent aristocrat Lota de Machedo Soares, a short visit expanded to cover 16 years, from 1951 to 1967.

And while Bishop always resisted the label 'female' poet, she nonetheless became the beneficiary of a movement that translated her from the narrow province of a poet's poet to a writer who was read in and out of the classroom, inspiring not only other women poets but future female academics as well.

The 1990s alone saw no fewer than nine critical monographs on Bishop published by female scholars. Bishop's first biographer was a woman, Brett Millier (1993), as was her second, Meghan Marshall (2015), a former student at Harvard; and although written much earlier, the first critical monograph on her had been written by the poet-critic Anne Stevenson (1966). Bishop was not just helped by the women's movement; appealing equally, if differently, to both sexes, she helped to expand a diversified readership for poetry in general. As the passages from 'The Moose' suggest, one doesn't need a college degree, let alone one from Harvard, to enjoy her poetry.

As part of her emergence, Bishop's conveniently compact canon of often casually perfect poems played an important role, as did her strong affiliation with another female poet, Marianne Moore, and a reticence that was not simply attractive in its own right but that invited critical and biographical commentary. Bishop, too, played into the hands of further generations of scholars. By saving many of her notebooks, drafts of poems, and epistolary materials, she helped, in effect, to 'curate' a future beyond what was already publicly available in print. These writings now constitute a remarkable personal archive. Held mostly at Vassar College, her alma mater, the materials, at the discretion of her literary executors, have been making their tantalizing presence felt in many quarters.

First came the publication of a large selection of her letters in 1994 that was universally praised, likened by one reviewer to 'discovering a new planet or watching a bustling continent emerge, glossy and triumphant, from the blank ocean'. Then the recovery and publication of her paintings in 1996, in *Exchanging*

Hats, of special interest given the richly descriptive, painterly element in her verse. The letters and paintings were followed a decade later, in 2006, by a large stash of unpublished and often unfinished poems, *Edgar Allan Poe & the Juke-Box*. And after that more letters. The complete correspondence between Bishop and Lowell, *Words in Air*, a riveting record of one of the great literary friendships, appeared in 2008. (It was subsequently made into a play, *Dear Elizabeth*, by Sarah Ruhl in 2012, and has recently been reprised starring Meryl Streep and Kevin Kline.) Then, in 2011, her correspondence with *The New Yorker* was published, telling us much about the grammatical habits that helped her achieve 'perfect pitch'. And, in the same year, after the death of her literary executor and partner Alice Methfessel in 2009, a cache of letters written in 1947 to her psychoanalyst, Ruth Foster, came to light as did the entire Bishop–Methfessel correspondence of some 500 pages.

Although limited to a single year, the Foster letters give voice to a number of intimate details involving Bishop's childhood and early adult life that have made their way into the criticism. These materials detail her continued anxiety over her alcoholism, which began in college the year her mother died and was never really overcome. They recount several crushes on girls at summer camp and boarding school as well as her unrequited passion for Margaret Miller, her Vassar roommate and one-time travelling companion in Europe. They also describe some of her dreams in relation to her poems, her thoughts about her body, the shame she felt over her attitude toward some of her poorer relations, and her fears as a young girl over a particularly abusive uncle George, the husband of her mother's older sister Maud, with whom she lived—behaviour that she fended off and later even managed to forgive, one sign among many of Bishop's remarkable resilience.

The sizeable Bishop–Methfessel correspondence, by contrast, sheds light on Bishop's later years. In 1970, Bishop met the 26-year-old Alice Methfessel, the administrative assistant at Harvard's Kirkland

House, where Bishop was staying. These letters, describing an older woman with a much younger lover, offer, in the absence of almost any surviving correspondence with Lota, the most intimate portrait of Bishop's daily life with another person.

By the early 2000s, there was suddenly much to say about this most reticent of poets, who was soon to arrive at celebrity status on a broad scale. International conferences, essay collections, more monographs proceeded apace, as Bishop's canon of writings swelled and seemed, in the process, amenable to a great many critical approaches and readers in the 21st century. Nova Scotian scholars made much of Bishop's extended family life and her maritime locale, in what has become a tug-of-war among regional readings of Bishop. Key West, where Bishop purchased a house in 1938 (now a literary landmark), and Brazil are the other major contenders. On both sides of the Atlantic, academics continued to trace her literary roots and routes, both deep and winding. Environmentalists found someone who cared about the world, not just the beleaguered self of confessional poetry, a movement Bishop generally deplored. Post-colonialists discovered a poet to critique and/or commend. Gender critics unveiled a 'queer' Bishop. Scholars of race examined, not always favourably, Bishop's long-standing interest in black lives. Her poems even appealed to the theologically minded, although she was an avowed non-believer. All the while, readers explored the fissure between the inner turmoil of Bishop's private life and the seeming serenity of the poetry.

On a more public front, Bishop became the subject of a widely released movie, *Reaching for the Moon* (2013), about her romantic years in Brazil, set largely in the beautiful modernist house in Petrópolis, on the outskirts of Rio de Janeiro, that Machedo Soares, a self-trained architect, helped to design and oversee its construction. This film was followed by another, an art film about Bishop's time at summer camp, *Welcome to this House,* by the experimental film-maker Barbara Hammer in 2015. More recently

Liza Wieland's 2019 novel, *Paris, 7 A.M.*—the title is taken from one of Bishop's early poems—gives a largely fictional account of her year abroad in 1937. In North America, only the mysteriously reclusive Emily Dickinson has exceeded Bishop in terms of a poet's cinematic and novelistic appeal, and for many of the same reasons.

Biographical beginnings

Thanks to a panoply of biographies, if Bishop's life no longer holds the mystery it once did, her poetry, like all great art, continues to do so, and the focus of this *Very Short Introduction* is to introduce new readers to her verse, the one truly inexhaustible 'story' of Bishop's life. From this perspective, biography is an important first step because places and people, heightened by memory and travel—those features of inner and outer geography so crucial to Bishop—are part of the fabric of her verse. Indeed, they ground her poems in the reality she always claimed to be describing.

Nova Scotia holds special relevance in this bio-geographical-literary scheme, and no account of her poetry can afford to ignore it. The maritime province was the home of her mother's family, the maternal line of descent that went back generations, while her father's line descended from Prince Edward Island; and, although Bishop was born in Worcester, Massachusetts, in 1911, the early death of her father from Bright's disease, when she was only eight months old, and the subsequent mental deterioration of her mother, who would be permanently hospitalized in Dartmouth, Nova Scotia, when Bishop was only 5, meant that she spent considerable time as a child in Great Village, Nova Scotia. She would often stay with her maternal grandmother in the house still standing near the town's centre and which serves as an occasional writer's residence and often the end point for numerous pilgrimages to her home country.

After her mother's hospitalization in 1916, Bishop lived most of the regular year with relatives in the USA—initially, briefly, and very unhappily with her grandparents on her father's side of the family in Worcester, Massachusetts, then with her maternal aunt and uncle in suburbs outside Boston. Great Village became a place for summer vacations and holiday visits, as she went off to boarding school at Walnut Hill (1927–30), then Vassar College (1930–4). In the later 1940s, Nova Scotia offered a source of personal refuge and poetic renewal as she faced a disintegrating relationship in Key West with her partner at the time, Marjorie Stevens, and a loss of direction and confidence in the immediate aftermath of the publication of her first book of poems, *North & South*, in 1946, which had been selected out of more than 800 submissions for the first annual Houghton Mifflin Poetry Prize Fellowship. Two of her most vividly evocative landscape poems, 'Cape Breton' and 'At the Fishhouses', would emerge from these ventures and appear in *A Cold Spring* (1955). Seeds were likewise planted for a much later harvesting of 'The Moose'—in 1972, when she finally finished a draft of the poem to be read at the Phi Beta Kappa ceremony at Harvard.

Bishop's family life had a large hole in the centre. She was an only child, an orphan, in effect, who suffered much of her life from frequent bouts of loneliness, asthma, eczema, and alcoholism. She thus required constant attention from her physician and lifelong friend Anny Baumann, and occasional hospitalization. (An allergic reaction to the cashew fruit on her arrival in Brazil, in fact, led to an extended visit with Lota that quickly blossomed into a romance.) Bishop's early life also included an extensive network of relatives, whose complex Nova Scotian strands require some careful decipherment by her biographers, in a rural community bound together at the turn of the 20th century by its regional, largely agricultural, often church-going, and—in the case of Bishop's family—literate identity. Bishop's mother was called Gertrude (née Bulmer or Boomer). Her sister Grace, Bishop's favourite

aunt, was 10 years younger than Gertrude. (Grace would marry a
Bowers, and it would be to Grace Bulmer Bowers that Bishop
would dedicate 'The Moose'.) There was also another pair of
alliteratively balanced sisters on the maternal side, Maud and
Mary; several 'uncle Georges' to untangle, as we discover in a late
poem called 'Poem'; and on her father's side—the wealthier Bishop
side from Worcester, from which she received the modest trust
fund that mainly supported her schooling and travel—a stern set
of grandparents and three surviving children, including Aunt
Florence, with whom Bishop lived briefly in 1917–18.

Bishop would eventually be buried in Worcester's Hope Cemetery,
with her parents, but only after a largely unplanned life that
included considerable travel in Europe, North Africa, and Mexico,
as well as along the eastern seaboards of North and South America.
The longest period of her staying in one place was the 16 years she
spent in Brazil with Machedo Soares. Their relationship brought
much happiness in the early years but grew to be more complicated
and strained over time, as Lota became increasingly involved in
the troubled political life of Rio as a commissioner of a new public
park, and Bishop sought escape in the provincial town of Ouro
Prêto, where she eventually purchased the second of her houses,
Casa Mariana (named in honour of Marianne Moore). Their
relationship ultimately ended in disaster. Bishop's letters from this
period in her life make devastating reading. An overworked,
depressed, and jealous Lota, against her doctor's advice, followed
Bishop to New York City in September 1967 and, whether accidental
or planned, died from an overdose of valium, leaving a distraught
and despondent Bishop ridden with guilt for years to come.

Bishop's gravestone in Worcester came to bear the words 'All
the untidy activity continues, | awful but cheerful'. These are
the concluding lines from 'The Bight', a poem in which the
unexpectedly rich detail of a busy Florida bay offers the lonely eye
of the writer some company 'On my birthday', as the headnote to
the poem reads. Bishop requested only the last line be carved on

her headstone, but Alice Methfessel found it too stark, so the preceding line was eventually added. Together the lines summon a view of daily life that tilts between emotional extremes, but rarely gives way to either, striking a clarifying balance in the face of things—a chief hallmark of Bishop's verse.

The Worcester connection appears rarely in Bishop's poetry, but when it finally does in 'In the Waiting Room', it carries all the weight associated with the return of the repressed. Written in a deliberately compressed autobiographical format, activated by her emotionally difficult return to the USA in 1967, when she began drafting the poem, 'In the Waiting Room' contains the only direct mention of Worcester among her published works. (Worcester does figure substantially in her unpublished prose reminiscence, 'The Country Mouse', which underlies the poem.) It is also the first poem in her final volume, the more personally immediate *Geography III* (1976), and it recalls from a child's perspective a disconcerting volcanic eruption of self-awareness in a dentist's office in Worcester three days shy of her seventh birthday. In the poem, her Aunt Florence appears as 'Aunt Consuelo'.

The power of the poem hinges on a layered understanding of the child's frightening identification of herself as female. An '*oh!* of pain' in the dentist's office, where Aunt Consuelo undergoes a procedure, gives birth, in the waiting room, to a young girl's painful dizzying, disruptive burst into self-consciousness:

> But I felt: you are an *I*,
> you are an *Elizabeth*,
> you are one of *them*.
> *Why* should you be one, too?

Yes, 'one, too', a female, that is, but as 'one' becomes 'two', the young girl, having been made uneasily aware of her body, her gender, and her connection to others, separates from the child and, assuming the adult poet's consciousness, comes into the 'night and slush and cold' of Worcester on the 'fifth | of February, 1918'. The date reminds us that 'The War was on', outside as well as inside.

In contrast to this single, wintry, wartime reference to Worcester, the province of Nova Scotia—the people, the maritime land and seascapes, the animals, the fish, and the birds—served as a recurring source of inspiration throughout Bishop's career. Northern subjects populate all four books of poetry. *North & South* (1946) contains 'The Map' and 'Large Bad Picture'. *A Cold Spring* (1955) includes a trio of Nova Scotian poems: 'A Summer's Dream', 'At the Fishhouses', and 'Cape Breton'; and *Geography III* (1976) includes two, 'The Moose' and 'Poem'.

Rather surprisingly, however, memories of Nova Scotia loom largest in her third book of poems, the substantially Brazilian *Questions of Travel* (1965), when her stay in that country prompted 'total recall' of Nova Scotia, including the most inspired of her short stories, 'In the Village', based on memories of her mother's breakdown in the context of a child's detailed recollection of her now perilous place in that rural community. The story serves as a structural hinge, as well, in the manner of Lowell's prose autobiography, '91 Revere Street' in *Life Studies* (1959). It links the Brazilian poems in the first half of the volume to the Nova Scotian poems that appear under the subtitle 'Elsewhere': most notably 'Sestina', 'Filling Station', and 'First Death in Nova Scotia'—along with several others that mention members of her extended family, her maternal grandfather in the delightfully poised 'Manners' and her Aunt Mary in the more anxiety-ridden 'Sunday, 4 A.M.'

'Sestina': 'another inscrutable house'

To look at one of these Nova Scotian poems in detail is to understand the brilliant art Bishop made out of a location, in this case one that bespeaks loneliness and absence. As with 'In the Waiting Room', 'Sestina' invites us to imagine a setting involving the child who became the poet. First published in *The New Yorker* in 1956, it is not, strictly speaking, an autobiographical poem, and there is a reasonable debate among readers about how much biographical information is needed in order to appreciate fully a poem as artfully conceived as this sestina. 'In the Village' clearly hints at the usefulness of family knowledge but such information remains optional because the sestina itself, at least in Bishop's hands, is so good at establishing a world of its own 'elsewhere'.

The strict form of the sestina requires the rotation of six carefully chosen terminal words over the course of six stanzas of six lines each, with a final stanza compressing all six terminal words into three lines, using two terminal words in each. It sounds complicated, and it is, but Bishop makes it seem as natural as the September rain that begins the poem. Here is the opening stanza.

> September rain falls on the house.
> In the failing light, the old grandmother
> sits in the kitchen with the child
> beside the Little Marvel Stove,
> reading the jokes from the almanac,
> laughing and talking to hide her tears.

What Bishop describes here is a cosmos within a cosmos that feels utterly real. (There really was a stove bearing the brand name 'Little Marvel'.) To sharpen the focus, she has reduced the length of the pentameter line usually associated with the sestina in English to a variably shorter tetrameter, that is, from five feet to four, or 10 syllables to eight in lines 1, 3, and 4. The six terminal words then give us the general setting ('house'), the principal characters ('grandmother' and 'child'), some of the properties relevant to the sparse setting and climate ('Stove' and 'almanac'), and the desperate mood ('tears').

The brilliance of the poem lies in the apparent simplicity of a mysterious story that unfolds in the course of these changing terminal words. This is a house but not quite a home. We don't know why the grandmother is crying, although she hints that her tears are environmental and seasonal, and are possibly connected, moreover, to a larger world of fate as foretold by the almanac. Since only the grandmother talks, we're also not sure of the exact bond between adult and child, the family ties behind an afternoon teatime ritual, although the child certainly wishes to please the grandmother by proudly showing her a drawing of a house. The grandmother is also always described with the definite article 'the', never the more intimate pronoun 'her', just as the child's gender is never specified, although we might suspect it is female. The carefully worked grammar is part of the distancing, the silence the sestina encases, as the house grows chillier, and the tears become ubiquitous. They show up, rather fantastically, in 'the teakettle's small hard tears', then in the tea in the grandmother's teacup, as if tea and tears possess some occult linkage in this part of the world; they appear again in the 'buttons' of the man in the picture the child is drawing of a 'rigid house | and a winding pathway', and, more magically still, as moons falling from 'between the pages of the almanac | into the flower bed the child | has carefully placed in the front of the house'.

Bishop has often been tied to surrealism, as we will see in Chapter 4, especially in her early poems, where images of dreaming and sleeping proliferate. But here the surrealism is connected to the everyday—those strangely mutable tears and the birdlike almanac, and the 'inscrutable house' the child draws, the last words of the poem. What does it all add up to? One obvious answer is the absent mother, the only person missing from the family puzzle if we allow the man with buttons as a stand-in for the father. But inserting this biographical key has the paradoxical effect of closing the door on the poem. It seems interpretatively reductive to fill in a blank that Bishop wants to expose, since the blank is what both grandmother and child are struggling with, in their different ways, as they fumble through the day: the grandmother trying to hide her tears, the child drawing first a 'rigid house' and then again yet 'another inscrutable house'.

Still, although lonely, the child is not quite bereft. Bishop is careful here, as we must be, but it is possible to see that the child bears a distant resemblance to the poet, who finds in the unrelenting ('rigid') form of the sestina the evolving potential for unfolding an inscrutable mystery in her own life, the absent mother that Bishop never again saw after she was hospitalized in 1917. It might seem, as it has to some, that by changing the title from 'Early Sorrow', as it was originally called, to 'Sestina', Bishop sought to distance herself from the difficult subject matter, treated here some 20 years after her mother's death in 1934. But it is also the case that we see in the generic title a reference to the ideal recursive form for registering sorrow, the grandmother's and the child's. And the generic title also hints at a further link: that in the child's repeated acts of making, we see an image of survival, a distant mirror reflecting the hand of the maker, the poet. *'Time to plant tears*, says the almanac.' The closing agricultural metaphor reminds us that September rain will yield fruit sometime in the future. Amid this bleak picture, there is a place for hope as well as sorrow, just as, upon reflection, an *'oh! of pain'* can be seen, in *Geography III*, as a productive part of growing up in Worcester.

'Filling Station' and 'a big, hirsute begonia'

Place, and the memory of it, are always crucial forces in Bishop's poetry. This goes for time spent in Europe as well as Florida, but two more Nova Scotian poems will deepen our understanding of this special place in her (he)art. Both poems are from the 'Elsewhere' section of *Questions of Travel* and illustrate some of the poetic virtues identified by Lowell, Merrill, and Heaney, in a context that also hints at the generative nature of Bishop's original family locale and her predilection, as we saw in her postcard, for an art that isn't perfectly straight but a touch whimsical and off-centre. And both, while hardly alone in this capacity, underscore what Bishop identified as 'the three qualities I admire in the poetry I like best': '*Accuracy, Spontaneity, Mystery*'.

'Filling Station', another mid-career poem, was first published in *The New Yorker* in 1955. It is probably based on memories of a gas or petrol station across the street from her grandmother's house in Great Village. An 'Esso' station once stood there; now it bears a different name, 'Wilson's'. But Bishop's description, while detailed, is familiar enough to have a recognizable generic feel, and appeal, to it. As with 'Sestina', the poem offers a microcosm of a family, one described from a first-person point of view, which might or might not be equated with that of the poet. It begins with the deliberately off-putting, anxious, but spontaneous exclamation, 'Oh, but it is dirty!' Then a father, wearing 'a dirty, oil-soaked monkey suit', appears with his 'greasy sons', as further details germane to the setting quickly emerge, familiar to anyone who has ever stopped at a family-run gas station.

Things, including the perception of things by a speaker, almost always undergo change in the course of a Bishop poem. Questions are rarely rhetorical but evidence of curiosity, of thought in process, revaluing the environment in a closer, usually more sympathetic light. And such is the case here. What initiates a swerve in a sympathetic direction is the recognition, amid the apparent clutter, of 'a big hirsute begonia' and the questions that follow from this observation.

> Some comic books provide
> the only note of color—
> of certain color. They lie
> upon a big dim doily
> draping a taboret
> (part of the set), beside
> a big hirsute begonia.

In its hairy bigness the begonia seems almost monstrous, but also slightly comical, as indeed its proximity to comic books might suggest. The small scene lends a touch of colour, of art, to the filling station, in the manner of a still-life. (Flowers on tables figure in many of Bishop's own paintings.) And as so often is the case in Bishop, the initially 'extraneous' comes to be seen as essential to the poem:

> Why the extraneous plant?
> Why the taboret?
> Why, oh why, the doily?
> (Embroidered in daisy stitch
> With marguerites, I think,
> And heavy with gray crochet.)

In contrast to 'Sestina', the reader doesn't need to discover or impose a missing mother. The speaker searches her out for us, drawn as she is to the embroidery (nestled within a parenthesis) and the apparently feminine hand that waters and orders this small universe:

> Somebody embroidered the doily.
> Somebody waters the plant,
> or oils it, maybe. Somebody
> arranges the rows of cans
> so that they softly say:
> ESSO—SO—SO—SO
> to high-strung automobiles.
> Somebody loves us all.

The final line seems so simple and yet is among one of her most mysterious in a stanza that is among her most enchanting—literally. In the repeated phrases and cadences, right down to the elongated, soothing label on a can of oil, Bishop invites us to wonder who this 'Somebody', this fairy godmother of gas stations, might be. To some she is the benevolent deity of Bishop's much admired George Herbert. To others she is less warmly received, the manifestation of Bishop's class consciousness and condescension (i.e. there is a 'somebody', a mother, who can love even this grease-stained family). To the more politically and ecologically minded, the 'somebody' is a sinister indication of the corporate takeover of the family by big oil. To the psychoanalytic critic, she is a compensatory sign for the mother Bishop lost, with the soft sayings of Esso cans (often interpreted as spelling a calming 'SO—SO—SO', or sew, sew, sew, although some have read it more alarmingly as an S-O-S) serving as a wishful response to the unheard mother's wrenching scream that spreads across the sky in 'In the Village', a scream provoked into being by a dress that didn't seem quite right in its stitching and colour.

Not all of these contexts are equally persuasive, but one more suggestion is needed. I think it is possible to read this gesture rhetorically, that is, on its own terms, as an evocation of hope by someone momentarily 'filled' by what she has seen. Bishop's poems often end in an open space, leaving us not so much reaching irritably after facts as simply recognizing, as in 'The Moose', that 'Life's like that'. A person, the speaker, moved to questioning the place of things, including her place in an initially foreign setting like a messy filling station, can sometimes arrive at a better, more generous understanding and say just this sort of thing.

'First Death in Nova Scotia'

The last Nova Scotian poem I want to consider here is the most exquisite of the trio. The poem's title, 'First Death in Nova Scotia', reminds us of the last line of a Dylan Thomas elegy that Bishop much admired, 'After the first death, there is no other'. Published a few years after 'Filling Station', in 1962, Bishop's poem is, like the other two, one of many triumphs of saying much in little. The poem is, pointedly, not a full-blown elegy. That will come 15 years later, in its own delicately intimate way, in the 1978 pastoral elegy

'North Haven, *In memoriam: Robert Lowell*'. Here, Bishop is remembering the experience of a small child's first encounter with death. In this case, the death is of another child, her little cousin Arthur, in an idiom tightly made for the occasion. The poem is a slender five stanzas, spoken by the child. Each stanza is 10 lines, each line three feet. The verse line suggests an affinity with the two somewhat fanciful poems that immediately follow ('Filling Station' and 'Sunday, 4 A.M.'), and the more chronologically distant and longer 'In the Waiting Room', in which the short line enables concentration on the revelation of a small child's expression and perspective.

The diction is also unusually simple and straightforward. It has some of the beguiling clarity of Andrew Marvell's 'A Nymph Complaining for the Death of her Faun'. Marvell's poem, cited in her notes from her year spent reading at the New York Public Library, is another diminutive poem about an innocent young girl, or nymph, mourning the loss of another innocent, in Marvell's case a faun or small deer. In Bishop's case the young child mourns the loss of another child, whose death gets curiously fused with the death of a loon. But Marvell's is a pastoral lament, a complaint. Bishop's is quietly, even stoically, set in 'a cold, cold parlor' overseen by 'my mother', in a room often thought to be the parlour in her grandmother's house. Bishop carefully depicts a chromograph of named English royalty on the wall: 'Edward, Prince of Wales, | with Princess Alexandra, | And King George with Queen Mary'. Chromography was a form of colour lithography popular in the early 20th century, and Bishop's reference to this process and its subject matter not only gives a dated, loyalist feel to the extended family occasion, frozen as it is in the author's memory. It also reminds us that the child's idiom, as we come to understand it, belongs to an altogether different register of speech from that of adult discourse.

Into this frozen world, the mother, 'my mother', makes an entrance. As part of the mourning ritual, she is said to have 'laid out Arthur | beneath the chromographs', and later, in the middle stanza, she speaks:

> 'Come,' said my mother,
> 'Come and say good-bye
> to your little cousin Arthur.'
> I was lifted up and given
> one lily of the valley
> to put in Arthur's hand.
> Arthur's coffin was
> a little frosted cake,
> and the red-eyed loon eyed it
> from his white, frozen lake.

It is a touching moment, the more so if we reckon that, apart from the reference to 'my mother's watch' in 'One Art', it is the only time Bishop's mother appears in the whole of her published verse. But her appearance is handled, notably, as part of the observed ritual itself. Bishop will not sacrifice the truth of the moment, as remembered, to a retrospective sentimentalizing of the kind she sharply criticized herself for doing with regard to her mother in her 1961 personal reminiscence, 'The Country Mouse'.

Quickened by the short lines, our own eye moves rapidly down the stanza to the fanciful figure of Arthur and his coffin as imagined by the child, pairing Arthur with the dead, red-eyed loon, 'shot and stuffed by Uncle | Arthur, Arthur's father', but still alive in the child's imagination. The genealogy seems purposefully dizzying as we follow the child into this rabbit hole of names. To the 4-year-old speaker, the shooting of the loon is as real as the death of the little cousin; and it is this swerve away from the ordering ritual of adults into the child's fanciful way of thinking that is so striking, and wrenching, as we enter the make-believe world of Jack Frost (not the adult-made world of chromographs) that the later Bishop, the painterly poet, clearly and movingly recovers:

Arthur was very small.
He was all white, like a doll
that hadn't been painted yet.
Jack Frost had started to paint him
the way he always painted
the Maple Leaf (Forever).
He had just begun on the hair,
a few red strokes, and then
Jack Frost had dropped the brush
and left him white, forever.

The difference between the two uses of 'forever' (the first, in parentheses and capitalized, linking it with the popular Canadian song of that name, draws our attention to the word) is so delicate as to invite a question: in a poem about death shouldn't the latter, as well as the former, be in capitals? But that would be too intrusive on the part of this poet. She remains faithful to the end to the child's story-book way of perceiving the world, even if that way of perceiving runs counter to what poet and reader know to be true.

The gracious royal couples
were warm in red and ermine;
their feet were well wrapped up
in the ladies' ermine trains.
They invited Arthur to be
the smallest page at court.
But how could Arthur go,
clutching his tiny lily,
with his eyes shut up so tight
and the roads deep in snow?

After the first death, there is no other. Or so it might seem after finishing this jewel of a poem. Howard Moss, Bishop's editor at *The New Yorker*, wrote about the poem's ending: 'The sudden release of the last line in a poem so compressed that each word is utterly necessary has the impact of a memory held under pressure which is suddenly allowed not to explode but to expand endlessly. Arthur's eyes are shut tight; outside all Nova Scotia lies dead in winter. But it is the word "roads" that has such large reverberations. Roads are where one goes; Arthur not only wasn't going; he never would be.' It is the recognition of this impossibility that the child's question finally admits, as the poem comes to its perfect-pitch close by rhyming the open, long vowel 'snow' with 'go' and thereby leaving, too, a small '*oh!* of pain' in the reader's ear.

Roads are where one goes, and for Bishop they took her in many directions as this chapter has suggested—not to mention extended periods of time spent in New York City or trips up the Amazon and to the Galapagos Islands. Nova Scotia will remain an important imaginative place for Bishop, but never a home, just as there will never quite be a mother in her poetry as in her life. There will be people, lovers, places, houses, and she will settle in, for a while, but she never fully put her feet down, except in verse. 'From narrow provinces | of fish and bread and tea...' ('The Moose'). There is always a part of Bishop that includes 'elsewhere'. And that 'elsewhere' leads to yet another new place from which she could also derive inspiration for her poetry. As she says in 'Questions of Travel', making a potent simile in the end out of an apparently ordinary scene sketched in the negative:

> But surely it would have been a pity
> not to have seen the trees along this road,
> really exaggerated in their beauty,
> not to have seen them gesturing
> like noble pantomimists, robed in pink.

Yes, surely. Who wouldn't want to be part of this fantastic venture?

Chapter 2
Formal matters

Bishop was a lyric poet through and through. She dabbled in other poetic genres, even exploring Ben Jonson's masques at one point. She wrote and published a number of short stories that have some of the virtues and subjects we find in the poems. One, 'In the Village', is a recognized masterpiece. She also translated from Portuguese a biographical memoir, *The Diary of Helena Morely*, which has its loyal readers. And she was one of the supreme letter writers (and a teacher of writers' letters as well) in the 20th century, a literary practice that spills over into and informs her poetry and has itself been the subject of scholarly and critical treatment. But lyric was her gift and legacy, even while, or rather because, she embraced many of the values associated with prose.

This chapter expands on the theme of much-in-little in Chapter 1 by offering an overview of the various kinds of lyric Bishop wrote—nursery rhymes, songs, ballads, recursive forms, such as the villanelle, the sestina, and the sonnet—in conjunction with a few of her more unusual practices with stanzas and lines, and a closing recognition of the importance of the concept of the baroque in her poetry. The chapter can only be gestural, not comprehensive, by the very nature of Bishop's accomplishment, since the one law she seems to have observed was never to repeat herself. There is no 'one' Bishop poem. This is a chief pleasure of her verse, its unsuspecting originality and high rate of success.

Still, a few general points can be ventured. Bishop seems to have conceived each poem as a kind of totality, a little cosmos or world made cunningly—to borrow a phrase from Donne that was much in the air for a poet growing up in the era of T. S. Eliot, whom she interviewed as a college student when he visited Vassar in 1933. And the more impersonal the poem the better, at least early on, when free verse was but one of many kinds of forms, rather than narrowly predicated, as it came to be seen with Lowell, on a psychological breakdown or personal expression. Each poem was to be a supple, finished object. It possessed its own distinct beginning, middle, and end, not so much marked for all time in the bold manner of, say, Shakespeare's Sonnet 55 ('Not marble nor the gilded monuments | Of princes'), but as written for the specific moment of its reading. 'Watch it closely'—the final line of her anti-monumental 'The Monument'—might be her motto.

No doubt Bishop's often slow rate of composition was a feature of her need to make each poem anew. Her fear of repeating herself, of coming out into the open without new clothing, fed into the sometimes long spells between poems, as she remarked at one point to her psychiatrist, Ruth Foster. '*Repeat, repeat, repeat*' was Lowell territory, she noted in 'North Haven', as was '*revise, revise, revise*'. But while Bishop might revise a poem in manuscript, sometimes going to extraordinary lengths as in the case of the 16 drafts of 'One Art'—her sole villanelle—she rarely repeated a complex form once it appeared in print. On the few occasions that she did, as in the cases of the sonnet and the sestina, the poems appear remarkably different or distant from one another. 'A Miracle for Breakfast' and 'Sestina' are separated in composition by nearly 20 years. The latter represents a slight modification of the form with regard to line length, but small matters are always large in Bishop, even if not all her poems are small. In almost every other way, the two sestinas are diametric opposites in setting, mood, and time of day. 'A Miracle for Breakfast' is a sumptuous, brilliantly lit, visionary feast by a young poet new to the game.

I can tell what I saw next; it was not a miracle.
A beautiful villa stood in the sun
and from its doors came the smell of hot coffee.
In front, a baroque white plaster balcony
added by birds, who nest along the river,
—I saw it with one eye close to the crumb—

'Sestina,' as we saw in Chapter 1, is a more stringent poem, older, wiser, and much sadder.

Sonnets, songs, and ballads

As for sonnets, the few she wrote either are relegated to the edges of her oeuvre or when they appear in print do so almost in disguise. Her early college efforts, 'Three Sonnets for the Eyes', are finished in the formal sense, but they remain among her 'Uncollected Poems'; and while these are conventional love poems of an Elizabethan kind, the sonnets that do appear in print about love take pains to distort or disrupt the form almost beyond recognition for largely mimetic purposes, as in the case of the third and fourth of 'Four Poems' from *A Cold Spring*, 'While Someone Telephones' and 'O Breath'. Or else they are on altogether non-amatory subjects, placed in separate volumes: a pair of sonnets involving a parable on drunkenness in a pigsty in 'The Prodigal' (*A Cold Spring*), or two sonnets glued together to form a single bleak poem on the Civil War in Washington DC, in 'From Trollope's Journal' (*Questions of Travel*). Both, too, bear Lowell's distinct inflections and mannerisms, his penchant for hyphenated adjectives ('glass-smooth dung' followed immediately by 'Light-lashed, self-righteous') and harsh realism, with the pentameter line often intensified by alliteration ('Their legs were caked the color of dried blood'). Even the gorgeous poem that concludes *North & South*, 'Anaphora', feels more like two poems in the tradition of matins and evensong than a variation on two sonnets that, upon close inspection, they turn out to be.

The most cunningly wrought of Bishop's sonnets lies at the far end of her career. Published posthumously in *The New Yorker* three weeks after her death, the simply named 'Sonnet' turns the form upside down and much else besides. It is a sliver of a poem. An instance of much-in-little, it inverts octave and sestet, and like a butterfly or hummingbird, it insists that we watch it closely, so quickly does it go by, flirting with almost every important aspect of Bishop's life—indecision, drunkenness, self-division, imprisonment, movement, mirrors, self-reflection, freedom, and at last, rather surprisingly, the possibility of her lesbian sexuality in the word 'gay':

> Caught—the bubble
> in the spirit-level,
> a creature divided;
> and the compass needle
> wobbling and wavering,
> undecided.
> Freed—the broken
> thermometer's mercury
> running away:
> and the rainbow-bird
> from the narrow bevel
> of the empty mirror,
> flying wherever
> it feels like, gay!

As with sonnets, so with songs, Bishop returns to the genre but never in quite the same way. Her keen ear for all sorts of music—classical, blues, samba, folk songs, church hymns, brass bands—led her to experiment with a brief suite of 'Songs for a Colored Singer' in *North & South*, with Billie Holiday in mind (issuing in a host of memorably syncopated rhymes), each poem using a different stanza. For the same volume, she composed 'Late Air', a belated (or 'late') reworking of an Elizabethan style 'air', or song, the kind that elegantly populate the world of the Jonsonian masques. In *Questions of Travel*, Bishop wrote her own exquisite

'Song for the Rainy Season' in what she called '*rumba* rhythm'. Six stanzas of 10 short lines apiece lightly alter the patter of rhymes in each to produce a mesmerizingly fluent revelation of love. In a different key, 'Brazil, January 1, 1502' conjures up the stern conquering spirit of the Portuguese with '*L'Homme armé* or some such tune', a reference to the ancient military hymn associated with the Latin Mass. In the 'Elsewhere' section of the same volume, 'A high *vox* | *humana*' is said somewhere to sing 'The gray horse needs shoeing'—a folk song Bishop seems to have made up—as part of the dreamscape of 'Sunday, 4 A.M.' More curious and unforgettable still is the ludic scene in 'At the Fishhouses' from *A Cold Spring* when Bishop, needing to delay her 'total immersion' into the 'Cold dark deep and absolutely clear' sea, imagines singing Baptist hymns, plus 'A Mighty Fortress Is Our God', to a listening seal, also 'interested in music'. But the musical *coup de grâce* goes to 'View of The Capitol from The Library of Congress'. A funny satire on the Air Force Band and the military more generally, 'the gathered brasses want to go | *boom—boom*'. Some of her own poems, in turn, were set to music by the American composer Elliott Carter in *A Mirror on Which to Dwell* (1976), although, rather surprisingly, he included none of her songs.

Bishop's supreme valuation of formal variety as a means to singularity was certainly one of the reasons she was drawn to George Herbert, and perhaps a reason why, rather surprisingly, she never quite embraced Emily Dickinson. Herbert was the master of formal invention in English, finding, it seems, a unique expression for each expostulation or 'ejaculation', whereas Dickinson, however singular in her sensibility and utterance, relied almost exclusively on the common ballad form descending from the Bay psalter. Bishop, too, liked the ballad form, with its closed rhyming quatrains, but more for reasons of narrative simplicity and speed than gnomic compression and assertion. One of her most charming early poems is 'Chemin de fer' in *North & South*. The title is French for railroad, hinting at the sense of brisk movement associated with the form. But the story that quickly unfolds seems fully American. Indeed it owes something to her summer camp experiences on Cape Cod, with even a touch of Robert (not Jack) Frost in the figure of the hermit. It begins, simply enough:

> Alone on the railroad track
>   I walked with pounding heart.
> The ties were too close together
>   or maybe too far apart.

Love, of course, is the understory here, as it often is in early Bishop. The heart pounds in excitement, but for potentially opposite reasons, as the pun on 'ties' suggests. We soon understand that it is a story about a hermit's unrequited love, of the 'ties' being 'too far apart'. Hoping for an answer from some unnamed other, the hermit fires off his gun in a sign of sexual frustration, while, we're told, 'The pet hen went chook-chook'. The startling ventriloquism is an early instance of Bishop's frequent play with animal sounds in her verse; and as the solitary hermit is a precursor of the exiled Crusoe in the longer, later poem bearing his name, so the comical 'chook-chook' will grow in that later poem into an eccentric mix of goat and gull cries, '*Baa, baa, baa* and *shriek, shriek, shriek | baa...shriek...*', as both source and sign of Crusoe's suffering on his island of maddening sameness. In the more restrained ballad, the simple 'chook-chook' signifies nature's indifference to the hermit's amatory plight, but we might also hear 'choke-choke', for the ballad ends with a hapless, throat-clearing shout:

> 'Love should be put into action!'
>   screamed the old hermit.
> Across the pond an echo
>   tried and tried to confirm it.

As one reader notes, the only echo that might possibly return from the old hermit's scream is the ghost rhyme, 'shun-shun'—unless we hear another from a Frost poem, 'The Most of It', which is also about failing to receive a counter-response of love.

When Bishop returned much later to the ballad form in 'The Burglar of Babylon' in *Questions of Travel*, she did so in another country, and for a completely different purpose. The roots of 'Chemin de fer' are essentially literary, perhaps stemming from W. H. Auden's modern revival of the form in the early 20th century, whereas 'The Burglar' belongs more to the ballad's association with popular writings as represented by Brazil's *literatura de cordel* ('literature on a string'), 'so named because they were produced as booklets, strung up, and sold from kiosks in cities of the Northeast'. (Bishop owned some of these *cordel* poems.) Her ballad refurbishes a story that was much in the Rio news about a local outlaw hero, Micuçú (pronounced mē-coo-soo, as she tells us), replete with vivid social and political commentary on the plight of the poor in their Babylonian favela (or ghetto) and the nervously dangerous, Keystone Cops-like soldiers (not police officers) chasing after their man.

Bishop said the ballad practically wrote itself, and one can see why, given the speed and rhythmic ease of the opening stanza:

> On the fair green hills of Rio
> There grows a fearful stain:
> The poor who come to Rio
> And can't go home again.

And the play with rhyme and point of view:

> They said, 'He'll go to his auntie,
> Who raised him like a son.
> She has a little drink shop
> On the hill of Babylon'.

And the simple action recounted alongside more complex acts of sympathy and reflection:

> Rich people in apartments
> Watched through binoculars

As long as the daylight lasted.
And all night, under the stars,

Micuçú hid in the grasses
Or sat in a little tree,
Listening for sounds, and staring
At the lighthouse out at sea.

Marianne Moore thought 'The Burglar of Babylon' Bishop's 'best'
poem, but probably, Bishop was fond of saying, because Moore
liked the moral that crime doesn't pay—whereas the ballad offers
much more than that. As Lowell intuited, it 'gives more of Brazil
somehow than your whole Life book', something recent criticism
keeps discovering, especially with regard to Bishop's often
conflicted perceptions of the Brazilian people and their culture,
drawn to the poor as she was but from an admittedly superior
position in the social hierarchy, an observer defining the observed.
As we will see, though, in part owing to her gender, Bishop saw
the world *differently*—through what Adrienne Rich memorably
identified as 'the eye of the outsider'.

'A bad case of the *Threes*'

A Bishop poem Moore did object strongly to was 'Roosters', one
of Bishop's most ambitious, formally insistent, and very best
early poems—'daringly messy' in Thom Gunn's words for this
floridly Floridian poem. (Bishop plays on this energizing
association of word and place two poems earlier in 'Florida'.) Its
44 stanzas are modelled on an unusual form she found in a
17th-century English poem by Richard Crashaw, 'His Wishes to
his Supposed Mistress'. Since 'Roosters' possesses a veiled
amatory setting of its own, Crashaw's title is not without
purpose, but it is the unusual tercets that thrilled Bishop and
eventuated in what she called, in a dispute with Moore, 'a bad
case of the *Threes*'.

'Roosters' is disposed into rhyming tercets, or '*Threes*', in this case lines of 4, 6, and 10 syllables each. As such, the poem offers an unusual portal into a more politically engaged Bishop than is often the case in her poetry. Published in March 1941, 'Roosters' responds to the outbreak of the Second World War by presenting a barnyard fable of sorts stemming from the early morning cry of a single rooster into multiple 'Cries galore' all about town. The poem offers a gendered critique of masculine war-mongering in the first half, answered, in the second half, on a quieter note with an elaborate account of the cock's religious iconography, constructed around Peter's threefold denial of Christ (Matthew 26:24). (Bishop rarely lets her learning show as much as she does in the second half of the poem.) Connecting the two parts is an amorous thread drawn from the aubade tradition involving two lovers waking in the morning, a favourite subject of Bishop's, in this case one that echoes Donne's 'The Sun Rising'.

The amatory theme will continue through the reference to Mary Magdalene, 'whose sin was of the flesh alone', whereas Peter's was of the spirit. It will then be touched on again at the end of the poem. Amid the gorgeous imagery of the sunlight 'gilding the tiny | floating swallow's belly | and lines of pink cloud in the sky', there is a whisper of concern that perhaps all has not gone perfectly with the lovers during the night. Some readers have felt that the sexually private displaces the war as political subject, but the poem's allegorical mode doesn't allow for easily containing the effects of battle. Bishop's domesticated roosters can be rendered with all the violence of fighter pilots:

> Now in mid-air
> by twos they fight each other.
> Down comes a first flame-feather,
>
> and one is flying,
> with raging heroism defying
> even the sensation of dying.

And one has fallen,
but still above the town
his torn-out, bloodied feathers drift down;

and what he sung
no matter. He is flung
on the gray ash-heap, lies in dung

with his dead wives
with open, bloody eyes,
while those metallic feathers oxidize.

So much for the glories of aerial combat: 'what he sung | no matter'. Time to turn in another direction, as Bishop does, toward 'old holy sculpture' for a story of hope.

Among the poem's many 'sordidities' that the fastidious Moore sought to expunge, including Bishop's reference to a 'water-closet', the older poet undertook to rewrite a cleaner version of the poem, without the offending tercets, and sent it to Bishop. Bishop made a few concessions to her mentor's criticisms. She changed the first word of each line into the lower case, for instance, but remarked, diplomatically, that 'I can't seem to bring myself to give up the set form'. The form, with its expanding lines and 'rattletrap rhythm', was crucial to the poem's '"violence" of tone'—what we might call 'Rooster's' intrusive subject matter in both the public and private sphere—so different from the element of colloquial immediacy, of readerly intimacy, that often characterizes her verse. Although Bishop never says as much, she must have had in mind the actual sound of the rooster cry. It is often three, sharply punctuated, expanding cries, a matter of duration reflected in the expanding lines rather than the way the sound is typically represented in print as a single sharp cry with three stresses, '**cock**-a-**dood**le-**do**'.

The immediate rustic setting for 'Roosters' was inspired by Bishop's time in Key West, Florida, an important period in her growth as a poet, but it's also difficult to think that her ear was not already tuned to the 'chook-chook' of chickens and the 'Cries galore' of roosters from her early days in rural Nova Scotia. The '*shush, shush, shush*' sound of cattle and people walking on wet sand in 'Santarém' is one of the many ways Bishop enlivens her verse by bringing it down to earth, in much the same way that her parentheses turn the formal into the informal, and strike a note of immediacy or spontaneity. The most famous example here is probably the parenthetical aside in 'One Art', when Bishop further infuses the villanelle, a form that thrives on repetition, with intimacy, dashed off (literally) in the spontaneous manner of an afterthought: '—Even losing you (the joking voice, a gesture | I love)'. Through typography, she encases or cradles a verbal gesture that she loves, what we think of here as intimate speech, now set off for both the speaker and reader to cherish.

So, too, she revelled in generically lower or more popular forms of literature, such as the ballad, nursery rhyme, parable, or beast fable. Making it new is not simply re-enacting a high-modernist credo, made famous by Ezra Pound, who is himself the subject of an extended remaking of a nursery rhyme in 'Visits to St. Elizabeths' and the grim shadows the form often contains. (The poem is based on 'This is the house that Jack built'.) We should also notice her funny comment to Moore: how a bovine Wallace Stevens, for all his tightrope walk with ideas, 'occasionally seems to make blank verse *moo*'. Humour as well as childhood memories help the young Bishop to imagine entering the largely modernist male fold. As does giving an occasional rap on the knuckles. While a student at Vassar, she writes to Donald Stanford, a graduate student in English at Harvard: 'And one thing more—what on earth do you mean when you say my perceptions are "almost impossible for a woman's"? "Now what the hell", as you said to me, "you know that's meaningless".'

Stretching the line

'Roosters' turns Crashaw's airy 'Ideas to his Supposed Mistress' earthward. The poem also occupies a pivotal moment in Bishop's relationship with Moore. It marked out her greater independence from the mentor whom she much admired. But their friendship continued, although now on more even ground. Moore actively championed the publication of Bishop's first book of poems, *North & South*, by Houghton Mifflin (1946). And Bishop returned the favour in her elaborate poem 'An Invitation to Miss Marianne Moore', in *The Quarterly Review of Literature* (1948)—reprinted near the end of *A Cold Spring* (1955)—and, in the same issue, the illuminating essay to be discussed in Chapter 3, 'As We Like It: Miss Moore and the Delight of Imitation'. Moore was also the subject of several other tributes written for college publications (Bryn Mawr, 1962, and Harvard, 1974).

Bishop's affection for tercets continued, too, but always with subtle differences, as we've come to expect. 'Wading at Wellfleet', 'Little Exercise', 'Under the Window: Ouro Prêto', and 'Pink Dog' are different not only from the more formally startling 'Roosters' but from each other as well. Bishop clearly liked the tercet's terseness, its concentrated phrasing (in the service of dog-trot pentameter in 'Pink Dog'), which is even more evident in her occasional use of the dimeter line. '"Half is enough"' she wittily concludes 'The Gentleman of Shalott', an early poem written in dimeter. (A later instance is 'Night City', again in a different format.) But she was not wedded to the idea of small forms, of being 'caught', as early, abundantly descriptive poems like 'Florida' and 'The Bight' remind us.

Much of the sought-after variety, the originality of her poetry, comes from how, throughout her career, Bishop stretched the line across and down the page. Widely across, as in the case of 'The Man-Moth', in which the long-lined stanzas contribute visually to the alienation effect of the urbanized human subject, fit for a Kafka novel, a practice of poetic de-familiarization that is further extended into the prose of '12: O'Clock News'. And narrowly down the page, again both early and late, in 'Jerónimo's House' and

'The Moose'. The single opening sentence of the latter poem, with its travelling bus and passengers, meanders mimetically through the Nova Scotian countryside for six stanzas until arriving at its first full stop in line 36. Although Bishop's literary models are many, her freedom with the extended short line, often playing sense against syntax, is reminiscent of William Carlos Williams's experiments with free verse (as in his deliberately slight 'This is just to say'), but worked out in the case of 'Jerónimo's House' on a more whimsically airy, domestic front, as the precarious placement of 'fairy' and 'perishable' suggest:

> My house, my fairy
>   palace, is
> of perishable
>   clapboards with
> three rooms in all,
>   my gray wasps' nest
> of chewed-up paper
>   glued with spit.

No need to tell her, à la Moore, not to capitalize the left hand margin. Bishop doesn't want anything as intrusive as 'Roosters' to interfere with the delicate effects of this loose grouping of decorations, of ephemera strung together into an intimate portrait of a domestic interior. Nor anything as off-putting as the block-like stanzas of 'Man-Moth'. Bishop's poem is an open invitation for the reader to enter into the creative life of the house and its rooms, its stanzas:

> Come closer. You
>   can see and hear
> the writing-paper
>   lines of light
> and the voices of
>   My radio.

Vertically slim 'lines of light' could be expanded and packaged into quatrains of simple, ballad-like construction ('Manners', 'Large Bad Picture', 'A Summer's Dream', 'Letter to N.Y.', 'Sunday, 4 A.M.', 'The Armadillo', each time slightly changing the line length or rhyme scheme), or into the more sophisticated measure of 'Twelfth Morning; or What You Will', with each quatrain concluding, in the manner of a Sapphic, with a short line, or into the obsessively detailed longer lines of the frantic 'Sandpiper'. And then opened up and expanded further, capaciously and freely, to give a sense of overflowing amplitude. Here is the beginning of 'Questions of Travel', responding to the overwhelming profusion of the Brazilian landscape, as a visitor, experiencing vertigo, might first see it:

Elizabeth Bishop

> There are too many waterfalls here; the crowded streams
> hurry too rapidly down to the sea,
> and the pressure of so many clouds on the mountaintops
> makes them spill over the sides in soft slow-motion,
> turning to waterfalls under our very eyes.
> —For if those streaks, those mile-long, shiny, tearstains
> aren't waterfalls yet,
> in a quick age or so, as ages go here,
> they probably will be.
> But if the streams and clouds keep travelling, travelling,
> the mountains look like the hulls of capsized ships,
> slime-hung and barnacled.

This may be Bishop at her most baroque, an adjective with a complex literary history that, in her case, can be traced back to a formative moment as a college student when she came across an important scholarly essay by Morris Croll, 'The Baroque Style in Prose' (1929), during a time when she was seeking to discover her voice. In its 'self-conscious modernism', the baroque style for Croll was the antithesis of the classical. Rather than favouring symmetry and balance of a Ciceronian order ('neither a borrower nor a lender be'), it valued the asymmetrical and spontaneous—notice the great variance in her line length—with Seneca as the model, and the prose of John Donne and Sir Thomas Browne as chief examples. Parataxis, rather than hypotaxis, abounds, a preference for adjacent phrases over subordinate clauses. 'Everything only connected by "and" and "and"', as she noted at the end of 'Over 2,000 Illustrations and a Complete Concordance'.

Not a thought, but a mind thinking

A single statement might set the theme, as above: 'There are too many waterfalls here'. It could then be amplified according to the pressure of thought, with 'the crowded streams' already overriding the first line in their hurry, and continuing in the subsequent lines of uneven length to arrive at an eventual period, or stop, only to have a dash pick up the idea in midstream, as it were, and begin another venture, turning thought back on itself. It is a heady, reflective move.

Croll gave this style a memorable formulation that struck a chord with Bishop, which she copied out, along with other ideas from Croll (and Hopkins), in the letter to Donald Stanford already cited.

> Their purpose (the writers of Baroque prose) was to portray, not a thought, but a mind thinking...They knew that an idea separated from the act of experiencing it is not the idea that was experienced. The ardor of its conception in the mind is a necessary part of the truth.

Bishop was especially drawn to Croll, she tells us, because of her discomfort with feeling bound by traditional metre. 'I can write in iambics if I want to—but just now I don't know my own mind quite well enough to say what I want to in them. If I try to write smoothly I find myself perverting the meaning for the sake of the smoothness.' Many years later, Croll's emphasis on portraying the mind thinking was still with her, even if his name was not within easy reach. But she certainly knew her own mind with regard to prosody. In the above passage, Bishop tacks to and from the pentameter line with great freedom, subordinating iambic feet to dactylic metre in the 10-syllable line ('**hur**ry too | **rap** idly | **down** to the | **sea**'), then stretching that line to a maximum of 14 syllables to set forth 'the pressure of so many clouds on the mountaintops'. She then returns, but with a difference (there's always a difference with Bishop), to the running dactyls of '**turn**ing to | **wat**erfalls | **un**der our | **very eyes**' by adding two syllables, in this case iambic. Finally, she radically curtails the line for a maximal sonic effect of closure by employing a spondee followed by two iambic feet. '**Slime-hung** | and **bar** | na **cled**' pulls the whole passage, with its cloud-like, fleeting sense of the dactylic '**tra**velling, **tra**velling', down to earth with an Anglo-Saxon thump—and registering with it a sense of mortality in the image of the mountains as 'capsized ships'. Here is not description per se, but the act of experiencing in the mind what the eye sees.

Croll's formulation points in two important but related directions in Bishop. By being drawn from prose, it helps to underscore Bishop's 'revolutionary' place as 'the first poet successfully to use all the resources of prose'. Readers usually have in mind here a variety of effects that contribute to making her verse sound 'natural': casually deployed phrases ('Well, I had fifty-two | miserable, small volcanoes I could climb'); errant thinking ('A light to read by—perfect! But—impossible'), when custom has led us to believe that thought in poetry should be more finished; parenthetical asides or dashes, as we've already seen; descriptions of the simple factual kind often associated with prose ('I caught a fish', 'Here is a coast; here is a harbor'); lists of many sorts; and a penchant for plain, unvarnished diction, as if she is taking the paint off words with each repetition ('He didn't fight. | He hadn't fought at all. | He hung a grunting weight').

The 'revolutionary' aspects also include not just noting local stylistic markers like those that we associate with prose but recognizing and responding to prose's broader rhythms that purposefully knit long stretches of her verse together: the repetition of like sounds in the above passage ('streams', 'sea', 'streaks', 'be', 'keep', with a return to 'streams', for instance), the calculated shift in line length to lend a variable movement to the whole (think of the long pause accentuated in the shift from the short to long *o*'s of 'soft slow-motion'), the echoing repetition of key words like 'travelling, travelling', in a poem bearing the title of 'Questions of Travel', in which questions and quest are intimately linked. Lyricism seems to persist, quite deliciously, right along with the extended list of questions: 'Oh, must we dream our dreams | And have them, too? | And have we room | for one more folded sunset, still quite warm?' Sunsets are the stuff of poetry; folded sunsets are what we pack in suitcases—in this case, however, in a near perfect iambic pentameter line that concludes with three rising stresses.

Croll's remarks also help to differentiate Bishop from Moore—who conceived of a poem as an elaborately constructed, finished artefact, 'a type of stylized collage'—by pointing toward an essential truth of Bishop's own poetry, gradually and variously worked out over her career, and in keeping with the more experiential aspects of American poetry: how to represent the ardour of conception, the mind thinking, and, as a consequence, the poem as a place to embrace the larger rhythms of change and open-endedness, of exploration and process. What were stylistically important were not the cumulative effects of symmetry and smoothness but the turns of thought associated with irregularities, with 'shifting gears', as she said much later in 'The Moose', with thoughts going forward by often backtracking, turning in and against themselves, opening up spaces and gaps in the thinking, as she does with increasing freedom in her later verse by frequently employing a device known as 'metanoia' or self-correction. It is one of her most indelible and attractive features, at once a sign of her modesty and her desire to be truthful to experience.

To some degree Wallace Stevens set the table for his modernist contemporaries when he wrote in 'Of Modern Poetry', 'The poem of the mind in the *act of finding* | What will suffice. It has not always had | To find: the scene was set; it repeated what | Was in the script' (my italics). There is a great deal of Stevens in Bishop; *Harmonium* was a book she said she had almost by heart; she elsewhere spoke of admiring the 'display of ideas at work' in his poetry. And there are lines in her poetry that, without the example of Stevens, seem unthinkable in their majestic play with perception: 'This celestial seascape, with white herons got up as angels, | flying as high as they want and as far as they want sidewise | in tiers and tiers of immaculate reflections' ('Seascape'). But 'if accuracy of observation is equivalent to accuracy of thinking', as Stevens himself observed in *Adagia*, it is Bishop, not Stevens, who best fulfilled the modernist ideal of poetry as the act of finding on a human scale in a world of familiar and not so familiar objects. Hers is the new script of a world felt not just in the imagination but with the eyes and fingers, a script that anticipates the improvisational and irresolute, the undoing of certainty so prized by postmodernist poets like John Ashbery, in poems that seem as grammatically fixed and meditated as any in the language.

Chapter 3
'The Armadillo', the art of description, and 'Brazil, January 1, 1502'

Setting the scene

Let's settle down with a single Bishop poem, one that Lowell liked enough to carry in his 'billfold and occasionally amaze people with it': 'The Armadillo'. The poem belongs to Bishop's mid-career, as does the photograph of her by Rollie McKenna taken during a trip to Brazil (Figure 3). 'The Armadillo' was first published in 1957 in *The New Yorker* and later collected in *Questions of Travel* (1965), and it has been a favourite with Bishop readers ever since. Lowell never ceased praising the poem. 'One of your absolutely top poems, your greatest quatrain poem', he noted in 1960, and he continued to carry 'The Armadillo' around for some years, mentioning it again in a 1964 letter. No doubt Lowell's enthusiasm stems in part from the significant role 'The Armadillo' played in the creation of 'Skunk Hour', the poem of his 'in a small voice' that brought *Life Studies* (1959) to a close. 'Skunk Hour' bore the dedication 'For Elizabeth Bishop'. And though Bishop would downplay her poem in deference to his—'it's only one fathom deep and "Skunk Hour" is five fathoms'—she nonetheless returned the favour by dedicating 'The Armadillo' to Lowell in *Questions of Travel*.

In the deferential knot tightening here, of poem with poem, poet with poet, one glimpses the larger story of a complex literary

3. Rollie McKenna, 'Elizabeth Bishop', 1954, in Brazil.

courtship that would continue throughout their adult lives and conclude only with Bishop's moving elegy to Lowell in 'North Haven'. But 'The Armadillo' has other features of interest besides encouraging a close-up comparison of two poets—or three poets, if we bring Marianne Moore back into the picture, as I will do. When Bishop speaks of her poem as 'only one fathom deep', she is voicing a continuing worry that her poems are often mere description, or in the case of 'Santarém', 'endless "description"'.

And, indeed, 'The Armadillo' is among Bishop's most descriptively enchanting. Think of its light, feathery beginning:

> This is the time of year
> when almost every night
> the frail, illegal fire balloons appear.
> Climbing the mountain height,
>
> rising toward a saint
> still honored in these parts,
> the paper chambers flush and fill with light
> that comes and goes, like hearts.

The scene is immediately imaginable, although what captures our attention is not the striking image of fire balloons, per se. Rather we're struck by the narrative simplicity of the occasion, the story line: 'This is the time of year'. The solitary image of the frail balloons sails delicately upward, across the space on the page separating the first two stanzas, with Bishop employing the easiest of rhymes and increasing the pulse with the extended third line, further leavened or aired by the simple, natural word order. The whole movement is then quietly infused with a flush of passion in the simile that brings the second stanza to a halt, as the alliteration of 'flush and fill' recollects, at a slight distance, the sound of the 'frailty' of the 'fire balloons'. Are we, we wonder momentarily, witnessing a love poem of some sort unfold? The poem immediately preceding, 'Song for the Rainy Season', might have us thinking in that direction, especially in its attention to the fragility of the densely ecstatic, amatory-ecological moment. But, no, the analogy is hard to sustain, as Bishop's meditative eye continues to pursue the upward course of the balloons:

> Once up against the sky it's hard
> to tell them from the stars—
> planets, that is—the tinted ones:
> Venus going down, or Mars,

or the pale green one. With a wind,
they flare and falter, wobble and toss;
but if it's still they steer between
the kite sticks of the Southern Cross,

receding, dwindling, solemnly
and steadily forsaking us,
or, in the downdraft from a peak,
suddenly turning dangerous.

In a variation on a comment by Lowell, we might say that, in following out their progress, Bishop is refusing to turn these balloons into symbols. She toys with this possibility, giving us some familiar named planets in Venus or Mars, but their place in this scheme is not to participate in an allegory of love and war; that possibility seems muted by the deliberately obscure reference to 'the pale green one'—whatever planet that might be. The purpose of this ascent into the heavens is to introduce an element of dreamy uncertainty into the poem as the personified balloons are blown about or else stand still, until, almost whimsically, 'in the downdraft from a peak | suddenly turning dangerous'. The phrase, with its plunging dactyls (**sud**-den-ly, **dan**-ger-ous), marks the poem's halfway point while also hinting at the drama to come.

Reticence and *Revelation*

'Many of your poems start obliquely', Lowell remarked, with this poem in mind, a strategy he rarely pursued, given his frequent practice of 'using oneself' as a point of departure, something Bishop rarely did. But he admired the freedom of imagination entailed in Bishop's method and made use of it in 'Skunk Hour'. And for the first five stanzas, we too share in the pleasure he describes, a pleasure that even continues into the first line of the next stanza, with its seemingly casual referent, until we arrive at the matter-of-fact image of the splattered egg:

> Last night another big one fell.
> It splattered like an egg of fire
> against the cliff behind the house.

Initially not even the fire's sudden proximity to the house seems to startle this speaker. 'I see the bomb in it in a delicate way,' Lowell remarked in 1965. Bishop's poem pre-dates US involvement in Vietnam, although Lowell, an arch-opponent of the war, may still have had it in mind, just as Bishop might have been recalling, in 1957, memories of the Second World War and subsequent fears of hydrogen bombs thereafter. But then reticence gives way to revelation, as it almost always does in Bishop, in ways that rarely cease to surprise:

> The flame ran down. We saw the pair
>
> of owls who nest there flying up
> and up, their whirling black-and-white
> stained bright pink underneath, until
> they shrieked up out of sight.

With this suddenly stirring depiction of violence, we might well rethink the poem's occasion. The saint 'still honored in these parts' refers to St John the Baptist, whose birthday is widely celebrated in Brazil on 24 June as a legacy of Portuguese rule; but the passage, now infused with sound and light, signalling confusion, and the owls' desperate desire to escape the chaos, invites us to think of another John, the visionary John of the Apocalypse. The suggestion is rarely noted, but how like Bishop to tease us with this other scenario, to layer suggestions of meaning without, in this case, becoming biblically heavy-handed. It is not scripture but nature, the destruction of nature in the figure of its creatures, that is her true subject in this poem, and yet she still honours, in her small way, the visionary moment associated with the Apocalyptic John. 'We saw the pair'—the enjambment across the stanza is perfectly timed—'of owls', who, escaping their home, fill up the quatrain, then shrieking, disappear 'out of sight'. Something terrible has happened, although rhyme and metre carry on.

At this point, 'The Armadillo' is surely more than 'one fathom deep'. And it is about to add another fathom with the quiet arrival of the title character:

> The ancient owls' nest must have burned.
> Hastily, all alone,
> a glistening armadillo left the scene,
> rose-flecked, head down, tail down,
>
> and then a baby rabbit jumped out,
> *short*-eared, to our surprise.

Bishop's eye manages to be scientific and poetic, filled with observation and feeling, and, to stretch the feeling further, the moment is one she shares also with another, a 'we', presumably her partner, Lota de Macedo Soares. Together the two witness the partial burning of their local habitat.

> So soft!—a handful of intangible ash
> with fixed, ignited eyes.

Just as it is difficult to ignore the apocalyptic John earlier, it's hard not to give this passage an autobiographical inflection. With the destruction of the owls' home, their nest, the armadillo marches forth, hastily and alone, resiliently and 'rose-flecked', carrying the images of its bright expulsion with it, 'head down, tail down'. (For all their lightness, 'nests' are loaded images in Bishop, as is her own sense of being an orphan wanderer.) And yet, now not alone but in the company of another person and together mutually surprised, Bishop cannot resist the sentiment embodied by the rabbit: 'So soft!' Is there any more tender utterance in all her poetry? (Perhaps her response to another animal, the dead hen in

'Trouvée'?) Here, Bishop leaves us uncertain whether the 'handful of intangible ash'—a nice paradox—refers to the rabbit's grey colour or its incineration; the image of its 'fixed, ignited eyes', a sign of its impending immolation or a reflection of its fiery surrounding.

That ambiguity might be sufficient for Bishop to conclude one of her early poems, which often thrive on riddles. But 'The Armadillo' has another step to go if its title is to be fully justified and, as it turns out, the poem as well.

> Too pretty, dreamlike mimicry!
> O falling fire and piercing cry
> and panic, and a weak mailed fist
> clenched ignorant against the sky!

'I am glad you like *The Armadillo*', Bishop wrote to Howard Moss, her editor at *The New Yorker*. 'I wish I wrote prophetic poems sometimes instead of the recollected kind', with 'The Armadillo' being the implied exception. And then she added, 'I think that perhaps the last stanza would look better italicized; what do you think? If it is, perhaps I could leave off the final exclamation point'. It did look better italicized, but she didn't leave off the final exclamation point. The move was unusual. Bishop rarely used italics ('Poem' is a notable exception), and almost never at the end of a poem, unless the italics designated a different mode of inscription, as at the end of 'Questions of Travel'.

Part of what is at stake is Bishop's awareness that the poem, so far, has not fully owned up to the occasion. The phrase '*Too pretty, dreamlike mimicry*' comments on the rabbit's innocently perilous situation, prettily reflecting, or mimicking, the hostile surrounding, but the phrase also reflects on the manner of the poem's representation. The quatrains so much admired by Lowell also reproduce a dream-like effect, a sentimentalizing brought to a head in the figure of the rabbit ('So soft!'). To go one step further, as we must and Bishop does, writing about the rabbit's 'fixed, ignited eyes' poses a challenge that couldn't be ignored regarding how to conclude the poem. The poem has arrived at a point of crisis, with revelation (or in this instance Revelation) pointing the way out: '*O falling fire and piercing cry*'. The prophetic voice, a rarity in Bishop, is the consequence of the poem's inner logic materializing in a speech act that draws attention to the desire for a more loaded language—what today we might call an activist's poetics.

By bringing out visually the 'cry' in 'mimicry'—the parallel placement of the two words in their respective lines makes the equation unavoidable—Bishop has added another fathom of depth to her poem, a new register. And in the final image of the armadillo's '*weak mailed fist | clenched ignorant against the sky!*', she adds another. A sign of the animal's helplessness, echoing the famous end of Matthew Arnold's 'Dover Beach' ('Where ignorant armies clash by night'), it hints at a further link between creature and poet, who, on this occasion, raises a 'mailed fist' of her own with a prophetic reckoning of the damage done to the immediate environment by the celebration of an ancient religious festivity. We reread sentimentality as environmental sympathy, and understand prophecy as including compassion for the weak.

Observing the observer

'The Armadillo' wasn't the ecological poem for Lowell it has become for many. For its more immediate literary roots in nature, and their ramifications, we need to turn to Marianne Moore, whose influence Lowell did recognize in the poem's title but also saw as going no further. 'A Moore name—though I suppose the armadillo is a much too popular and common garden animal for her—for an out-of-doors, personally seen and utterly un-Moore poem.' Today we might not readily view the armadillo as a common garden animal, although in the context of Moore's often exotic zoological excursions it might seem so. But Lowell's remarks hint at profound differences between Moore and Bishop. A glance at any number of Moore poems illustrates these points of similarity and difference but perhaps none better than her often anthologized 'The Pangolin', so called from the Greek to designate a species of scaly anteaters living in Africa or Asia. Here are the poem's opening lines:

> Another armored animal—scale
>   lapping scale with spruce-cone regularity until they
> form the uninterrupted central
>   tail-row! This near artichoke with head and legs and grit-equipped
>   gizzard,
>   the night miniature artist engineer is,
>   yes, Leonardo's—da Vinci's replica—
>   impressive animal and toiler of whom we seldom hear.

One can see why Bishop was immensely attracted to Moore as an original voice among modernists. Moore's free-wheeling lines represented a new way of looking, of conceiving a poem, in this case with a strange animal in its focus. 'As far as I know', Bishop wrote in a 1948 issue of the *Quarterly Review of Literature* honouring her mentor, 'Miss Marianne Moore is The World's Greatest Living Observer'. Moore is even better, Bishop goes on to say, than 'our greatest poet', Shakespeare, and offers proof by way of identifying (rather unfairly) Shakespeare's habit of describing animals as 'preconceived notions and over-sentimental' with a quotation from the melancholic Jaques's famous 'wounded deer' speech in the pastoral comedy *As You Like It*.

What drew Bishop to Moore among other things was Moore's 'immediacy of identification' with the creatures she was observing and representing in verse, but without condescension, 'without "pastoralizing" them as [the critic] William Empson might say, or drawing false analogies'. And in this 'unromantic, life-like, somehow *democratic*, presentation of animals' Moore helped Bishop (who was also aided by her reading of Darwin) to write about animals and, more broadly, nature from a sympathetic but not exclusively human-centred perspective: to see in nature something whose purpose was not to validate the seeing eye of the observer—and in the old hierarchy that observer was almost always male—but something with its own distinct habits and right to be. In this, both Moore and Bishop represent a clear departure from Romantic visionary poets such as Wordsworth, as well as American transcendentalists and sceptical naturalists in the tradition of Thoreau and Frost respectively. They also anticipate many of the concerns of today's ecologists worried about the environment.

But the two poets' means of representation differed greatly. Bishop hints at this matter when she notes in the same essay that Moore, in giving herself 'up entirely to the object under contemplation', can '"go on" so that there seems almost to be a compulsion to this kind of imitation'. And so 'The Pangolin' goes on and on, for nearly 100 lines, yoking together a vast number of heterogeneous images of a Donne-like order on a topic one might find in a collector like Sir Thomas Browne. Bishop's wariness here, her recognition of 'a compulsion' that must be resisted (surely true for Bishop as well), stems from and indeed helps to fuel a basic belief that undergirds her poetics.

> I do not understand the nature of the satisfaction a completely accurate description or imitation of anything at all can give, but apparently in order to produce it the description or imitation must be brief, or compact, and have at least the effect of being spontaneous. Even the best *trompe-l'oeil* paintings lack it, but I have experienced it in listening to the noise made by a four year old child who could imitate exactly the sound of the water running out of his bath.

Moore's poems, not so much in the specific image but in their totality, tend toward the artfully static, the two-dimensional, whereas Bishop is always trying to infuse description with narration or movement of thought, to add depth, which is why she so often fretted over its possible lack, and her own place as merely this or that kind of poet—'a minor female Wordsworth', a poet too much known for a particular subject (like Brazil), a poet identified through a single affiliation with another author (including Marianne Moore), or a single school of authors, especially those of her own sex. Bishop's often-stated admiration for that unusual trinity of poets—Herbert, Hopkins, and Baudelaire (with Baudelaire being the odd poet out)—was one means to keep multiple strands of influence in play, and her own independence alive.

In the case of 'The Armadillo', depth, three-dimensionality, is a matter of timing, of putting the animal in the right place, as if the poem were not a picture but an act of depicting, an exploration of how we arrive at seeing a particular subject. We sense we know the animal because of the environment it inhabits. Here, the armadillo makes a late, seemingly spontaneous appearance on the scene, as will be the case again, although even more startlingly, with the moose in 'The Moose'. The armadillo is then lightly but exactly described, as is true with the rabbit that precedes 'him' (the pronoun is Bishop's), and then in line only with the needs of a larger, already established narrative that is essentially moral rather than political. (Note that, once mentioned, Bishop doesn't return to the subject of the balloons' being illegal.)

This is a poem that describes the fragile place not of fire balloons alone, as it turns out, but, more importantly, of animals in Brazil and beyond, who also come and go, 'like hearts'. Although more than a country mile separates Bishop's small sketch from the larger environmental disasters now only too frequently reported around the world, we might glimpse an eerie point of continuity in a recent issue of *The New Yorker*, the magazine in which Bishop once so frequently appeared. A Canadian ecologist describes the battle being lost for green land in the Amazon: 'It's like the Four Horsemen of the Apocalypse have been let loose.' The Four Horsemen, of course, appear in Revelation 6.

Description and depth

Bishop had a nearly infinite number of ways to turn 'pure' description into something else, something more (or, following Lowell, *not* Moore), and it is one of the key reasons why readers of all stripes keep returning to her poetry. To add depth to our own discussion, I'd like to pursue this observation involving depth in one other poem, 'Brazil, January 1, 1502', a textbook example of her going deeper into a subject that mattered a great deal to her.

The poem, from *Questions of Travel* (1965), is routinely described by critics as 'great' or 'beautiful' (with Lowell again leading the way). It stands out in Bishop's canon of published verse as the only poem to use a title to place its subject in a specific—and in this case distant—historical context. (Bishop was fond of diurnal, not historical titles, as in 'Paris, 7 A.M.' or 'Twelve O'clock News'.) The year 1502 is not the date of the first Portuguese landing in Brazil. The original discovery of Brazil, as Bishop knew, is usually dated two years earlier and assigned to Pedro Álvarez Cabral, but the later dating links her own approximate arrival in Brazil with the arrival of the Portuguese 450 years earlier. To make the potential parallels (and the differences) even more pronounced, Bishop does an unusual thing: she places the date, '*January, 1952*', at the end of 'Arrival at Santos' in *Questions of Travel*, whereas in the poem's first appearance, at the end of *A Cold Spring*, she had left the poem undated.

Why is Bishop so keen on suggesting this connection? In part, because it helps to fulfil an open promise she makes at the end of 'Arrival at Santos': not to remain a tourist, however much fun the experience is with 'Miss Breen', but to be a traveller, an explorer, by penetrating more deeply into the subject of this vast country: visually, historically, sociologically, psychologically, racially, anthropologically, literarily, and erotically. But on her own terms, as we've already seen in 'The Armadillo', not those crudely employed in her Time-Life *Brazil* (1962). The last line of 'Arrival at Santos' reads, 'we are driving to the interior', a line that sets up multiple expectations regarding the subsequent poems and their mini-histories of this new country she is discovering.

In the case of 'Brazil, January 1, 1502', we follow a Janus-faced connection between present and past, new and old, between the touristic now (as a legacy of 'Arrival') and the colonizing then (as a feature of the title and continued in the opening salute). 'Januaries, Nature greets our eyes | exactly as she must have greeted theirs.' This is the abrupt beginning of the poem, a proposition supposing a likeness, so long as innocent nature is the poem's sole subject, as it is in the first stanza. The pronoun 'our' also implicates the reader in the process of 'driving to the interior' in this poem—in the direction, that is, toward the eventual heart of darkness that discovers the first Portuguese explorers to be predacious conquerors.

'Brazil, January 1, 1502' is drawn from what Bishop calls 'the cold hard mouth | of the world' in 'At the Fishhouses'. It is a textbook instance, as I suggested, of her going deeper into a subject over the course of three successive stanzas; of her delving—to redeploy an idiom from 'The Map'—into the shadows that inhabit the shallows. In the first stanza, she presents the shallows, innocent nature as it might have appeared to the voyagers on first landing and can be made to appear to the later reader through art, as Milton understood in describing sinless Eden in *Paradise Lost*. Flourishing with nouns, Bishop's descriptive powers with colour are equal to the visual rarity of the original occasion:

> monster ferns
> in silver-gray relief,
> and flowers, too, like giant water lilies
> up in the air—up, rather, in the leaves—
> purple, yellow, two yellows, pink,

rust red and greenish white;
solid but airy; fresh as if just finished
and taken off the frame.

The description here, of nature being made into art, 'fresh as if just finished | and taken off the frame', also neatly realizes in verse the first half of the epigram Bishop chose for the poem from the art historian Sir Kenneth Clark: 'embroidered nature...tapestried landscape', quoted from his book *Landscape into Art*, the title also included in the epigram.

The second half of the Clark epigram, 'tapestried landscape'—together the chosen phrases make up a perfectly balanced pentameter line—underscores the shift in perspective in the second stanza, from present to past and the shadows that underlie the shallows. Bishop renders the Brazilian landscape as it might have appeared in a Portuguese tapestry woven around the time of Brazil's discovery, a description now perceived through an old world allegorical lens of Augustinian Christianity, steeped in lessons of the Fall, fiercely attentive to 'Sin' and (repressed) sexuality, giving life, as it were, to the earlier 'monster ferns': 'The lizards scarcely breathe; all eyes | are on the smaller, female one, back-to | her wicked tail straight up and over, | red as a red-hot wire'. 'All eyes' refers to lizards, but also perhaps to the original viewers of the tapestry and most certainly to the readers of the poem. It is an unsettling moment, the 'red-hot wire' of the tail suddenly particularized in the context of a sexualized gaze. A Darwinian description of mating collides with the moralizing discourse of theology.

In the third stanza Bishop goes deeper still. She enters into history as imagined in 1502. The scene is introduced by a sudden turn, 'Just so', with 'Sin' now surfacing in the figure of the Portuguese conquerors. As with the earlier 'monster ferns' becoming dragons, so now with the men becoming crucifying monsters, 'hard as nails'. The poem stretches in an epic direction that doesn't quite deliver the heroic—the men are also 'tiny as nails'—or even the mock-heroic (issuing in laughter), but rather something more tonally complex and unstable, like the Lilliputian underside of epic, as if Bishop were rewriting, in her own terms, a scene from the most famous of Portuguese heroic poems, *The Lusiads* (1572), by Luís Vaz de Camões, celebrating Vasco da Gama's voyage to India. (The epigraph to *Questions of Travel*, dedicated to Lota, is from one of Camões's love sonnets.)

> Just so the Christians, hard as nails,
> tiny as nails, and glinting,
> in creaking armor, came and found it all,
> not unfamiliar:
> no lovers' walks, no bowers,
> no cherries to be picked, no lute music,
> but corresponding, nevertheless,
> to an old dream of wealth and luxury
> already out of style when they left home—
> wealth, plus a brand-new pleasure.
> Directly after Mass, humming perhaps
> *L'Homme armé* or some such tune,
> they ripped away into the hanging fabric,
> each out to catch an Indian for himself—
> those maddening little women who kept calling,
> calling to each other (or had the birds waked up?)
> and retreating, always retreating, behind it.

'How I envy the historical stretch at the end, so beautifully coming out of the vegetation,' Lowell remarked in 1965. And surely he is right to admire the transition out of the foliage into history, just as in an earlier letter he admired the tonal complexity of this part of the poem. But Lowell is otherwise silent on the matter of sexual conquest and colonization, in contrast to much current criticism that steers us toward the subject of rape on many levels in this poem. These include the colonialist subjugation of Brazil to Portugal, the new world to the old, with imperialism as creaky and threatening then as now. In the minds of some, the critique involves Bishop, the poet, too, as a potential appropriator of the spoils herself, whose career in the USA was advanced by her Brazilian subject matter. The last is one Bishop herself recognized, but can be overstated. What alternative was open to her? Leave Brazil? Not write? Or, as she chose to do, write about her subject with knowledge and sympathy, enhanced by the gendered eye of the outsider? As she says at the end of 'Questions of Travel', '*Continent, city, country, society:* | *the choice is never wide and never free*'.

The unusual phrase 'they ripped away into the hanging fabric' opens up many possibilities on this violent front. Along with underscoring the behaviour of the soldiers driven by the desire for 'a brand-new pleasure', it sets in motion thoughts regarding the Philomel story from Book 6 of Ovid's *Metamorphoses*. Revisited by Shakespeare in *The Rape of Lucrece*, the incident is lightly touched on here in the attention to tapestry and the odd parenthetical question at the end about the calling of women being perhaps the sound of birds waking up. (In Ovid, a tongue-less Philomela weaves the story of her rape by Tereus in a tapestry; she and her sister Procne then escape the raging Tereus by being transformed into birds, as happens to him as well.) The echo hints at that long cast of women forced to retreat to save their lives, if no longer the fabric of their virginity: 'retreating, always retreating' but not quite lost to sight, as the fable of Philomela, 'flowing and flown', reminds us in its many later iterations, including this one, heroically 'drawn'—in several senses of that word—'from the cold hard mouth | of the world' ('At the Fishhouses').

Bishop herself was characteristically modest about the poem. In responding to Lowell's initial burst of enthusiasm, she remarked: 'I am so glad you liked the New Year's poem. I think it is a bit artificial, but I finally had to do something with the cliché about the landscape looking like a tapestry, I suppose.' And so she does. Giving local habitation and considerable invention to the airy nothing of cliché in the first two stanzas, she then altogether tears through it in the final section, appropriating one kind of violence (sexual) through another (artistic), to reveal a world long familiar to the reader but now seen mysteriously anew, as only the closely woven fabric of her marvellous art can do. For Bishop the explorer, coming to terms with the cheerful natural landscape means coming to understand the sometimes awful footprint of human history.

Chapter 4
Poetry and painting

This chapter seeks to extend Bishop's unusual powers of observation in a direction readers have long recognized as a special feature of her poetry: its relationship to painting and, as a corollary, what is often referred to as her poems' painterly quality and the subject of looking more generally. And a good place to begin is with a 1955 letter Bishop wrote to Randall Jarrell. Jarrell had glowingly reviewed *A Cold Spring* (1955), which also included the poems from *North & South* (1946), in *Harper's Magazine*, observing at the outset that 'her *Poems* seems to me one of the best books an American poet has ever written: the people of the future...will read her just as they will read Dickinson or Whitman or Stevens, or the other classical American poets still alive among us'. That little word 'ever' jumps off the page in all its certainty, as does the mention of a single national affiliation that wraps Bishop into an American canon of authors. Then he adds, in parenthesis, 'the poems are like Vuillard or even, sometimes, Vermeer'.

Of course Bishop was pleased. She responded from Brazil with the kind of immediacy that makes reading her letters an event on its own.

> [Your review] has made me so happy that I really can't put off
> writing you a note about it any longer. Particularly living so far away

now, and having only three or four friends here who read English poetry at all, to show anything to—and they are all prejudiced so much in my favor, having read nobody else alive, to speak of! Sometimes I have the odd sensation that I am writing solely for you—which, after this piece, I don't mind a bit but shall try to relax and enjoy. I couldn't believe it at first, honestly—had a ridiculous fancy that it must be a misprint prolonged—shed a few tears—(they come from taking cortisone, partly—one gets highly emotional)—but I would have felt like shedding them even without the cortisone. I still, from the bottom of my heart, honestly think I do NOT deserve it—but it has been one of my dreams that someday someone would think of Vermeer, without my saying it first, so now I think I can die in a fairly peaceful frame of mind, any old time, having struck the best critic of poetry going that way…

We can certainly see why Bishop valued spontaneity in poetry. When she eventually arrives at Vermeer, she has already taken her reader rapidly through much 'lived experience', her reader in this case being most emphatically the recipient of this letter, Randall Jarrell, who, were it not already the case that he was the most revered (and feared) critic of poetry of his day, would almost certainly feel as if this were so. Johannes Vermeer was Bishop's big little secret that she now shares with another, on her way to heaven. Or to another thought (they're almost the same thing, for this spontaneously thinking person). Edouard Vuillard had also been recently in her head in a more practical way, she tells Jarrell, as a model for effects she was seeking to create in some short stories and a play she was working on.

Bishop's letters are filled with overflowing moments like this. She will touch on an idea here, describe a person there, interrupt a thought only to pick it up later, note a detail that will mean something special to the recipient, in prose that is unfailingly supple and lucid. Here the Dutch Vermeer and the French Vuillard offer an open-ended visual perspective into her poetry.

No paintings are specifically named but parallels are suggested, and readers have been quick to run with them, sometimes quite brilliantly:

> Bishop was Dutch in her love of curiosities locatable in time and place (a hen run over, in summer, on West 4th Street); of genre scenes (Faustina and her mistress, the 'Filling Station' attendants) or single figures at their daily tasks (the 'sad seamstress', the boy Balthazár, the old netminder outside the fishhouses); of microscopic close-ups and lucid distances ('I can make out the rigging of a schooner | a mile off'); of maps, which, as [Svetlana] Alpers puts it, show us 'not land possessed but land known in certain respects'; and in her general avoidance of allegorical framework as well as of the rhetoric that corresponds, perhaps, to those wonderstruck figures gesturing from the edge of a nativity or a martyrdom, as if the viewer wouldn't otherwise know where to look or what to feel.

James Merrill is speaking about the Dutch 'realist' painters of the 17th century, celebrated for their art of describing, of which Vermeer was the most accomplished and, like Bishop, the most discriminating. He painted only a small number of works. But as her reference to Vuillard indicates, Bishop's artistic affinities and interests can't be simply bound, even by comments as complex and perceptive as these. Vuillard takes us into the 20th century, as does Bishop's 'Roosters' letter to Marianne Moore in which she refers to 'the violent roosters Picasso did in connection with his *Guernica* picture'. Bishop then adds, for good measure, that the '"violence" of tone…makes me feel like a wonderful Klee picture I saw the other day, *The Man of Confusion*'. Both references allow Bishop to fend off Moore's criticism of her poem, and the one to Paul Klee, issuing in an invitation for Moore to see the exhibition with her, helps to smooth over whatever feathers of Moore's Bishop might have ruffled in the process. Klee, it should be said, was a special favourite of Bishop's. He appears occasionally in her letters, one time as an example of 'that strange kind of modesty that I think one feels in almost everything contemporary one really likes—Kafka, say, or Marianne [Moore], or even Eliot, and Klee and Kokoschka and Schwitters...Modesty, care, *space*, a sort of helplessness but determination at the same time.' Surely Bishop is also speaking about herself.

As these passing references suggest, Bishop was comfortable conversing about art, even occasionally moving in and around artists and the art world more generally, although always aware of her distance from it. Her wealthy Vassar College classmates and travelling companions Margaret Miller and Louise Crane were part of the New York scene that sometimes included Bishop. So, too, was the painter Loren MacIver, a lifelong friend (married to the poet Lloyd Frankenberg), whose paintings Bishop much admired, and sometimes acquired as gifts, as MacIver apparently did hers. It was through Miller that Bishop deepened her knowledge of Schwitters and his concern with collage; and it was in the company of Louise Crane, in Key West, that Bishop invited a folk artist, Gregorio Valdes, to paint a picture of their house, an episode recalled in the memoir of him and his paintings that Bishop published in the *Partisan Review* in 1939.

Bishop's time in Brazil also brought her in touch with a variety of artists and architects, local as well as from abroad, the most notable perhaps being Alexander Calder, the celebrated inventor of the mobile. He and his wife were friends of Lota's and, as Bishop describes them, colourful house guests. A Calder mobile in Lota's house near Petrópolis is pictured in one of Bishop's paintings (Figure 4). Bishop's letters from this period are likewise peppered with lively vignettes that reflect something of her own preferences and taste. Visiting the 'Biennale' in São Paulo—'Thousands of abstractions—horribly depressing after a few hours—but a few very good things—folk stuff from Bahia'—Bishop reports being in the company of works by Francis Bacon and Mies van der Rohe and the famous art critic Meyer Schapiro: 'I'd never met him, but got up my courage and accosted him in the

4. Elizabeth Bishop, *Interior with Calder Mobile*, undated, watercolour and gouache.

hotel, and he couldn't have been nicer.' The story gets better and more gossipy (she is writing to her New York friend Pearl Kazin): 'Just after Schapiro who should arrive at the house one day (I was in the shower!) with our architect but [Richard] Neutra and his wife. He is very handsome but must be a bit gaga. He squeezed me tenderly to his side, upon introduction, peered into my eyes, and asked me, "Do you know who I am? Have you ever heard of me?"'

How Bishop's considerable familiarity with art enters into her poetry is both a simple and complex matter. She was herself an amateur painter in a distant line of family painters and occasionally professed the wish that she had been born a painter rather than a writer. She worked mainly in ink and watercolour on a small scale, often 'on sheets of paper the same size that one might write a poem on'. She liked painting interior domestic scenes, buildings, and landscapes (rather than portraits), with a

5. Elizabeth Bishop, *Interior with Extension Cord,* **undated, watercolour, gouache, and ink.**

preference for flat, colourful surfaces and wiggly lines that give many of the works a light, slightly whimsical feel (Figure 5). Her paintings are well described as giving the impression of a calculated simplicity and an impersonation of naivety. They are not, in other words, to be confused with the untrained efforts of Valdes, whose work Bishop sometimes admired because of its indifference to notions of verisimilitude and the occasional accidental triumphs it produced: 'a peculiar and captivating freshness, flatness, and remoteness'. Her paintings also share some of the values and subject matter of the poems: a stove in one, flowers in another, a cabin on a boat (Figure 6), a tea service,

6. Elizabeth Bishop, *Cabin with Porthole*, undated, watercolour and gouache, 6 × 6 inches.

landscapes of Nova Scotia and Brazil, but little of their depth and refinement.

Although of considerable commercial value today, the 40 or so paintings that have come to light were done for her own pleasure and often meant as private gifts for friends and lovers, not for showing in public or collecting. Some bear scribbles of a personal kind: 'for Lota, Longer than Alladin's [*sic*] burns, | Love, & many Happy returns'.

Colour

Still, Bishop's practice as a painter, as well as her painterly eye for detail, is borne out in any number of ways in the poems, especially in her attention to the materiality of the artistic medium. We've already noted in Chapter 3 the 'simple web, | backing for feathery detail' of tapestry in 'Brazil, January 1, 1502'. But we've said little about the rich effects of colour and their patterns that make her poems, in their vividness, seem to defy the fact that we're only reading words on a page. 'Tilted above me', says the speaker in 'Manuelzinho', 'your gardens | ravish my eyes. You edge | the beds of silver cabbages with red carnations, and lettuces | mix with alyssum.' And so with the poems, not just those of the warm floral south but of the cold monochromatic north. Here are a few memorable lines from 'At the Fishhouses', awash in the cool silvery light of a single colour and crucial to establishing the sombre mood of the poem:

> All is silver: the heavy surface of the sea,
> swelling slowly as if considering spilling over,
> is opaque, but the silver of the benches,
> the lobster pots, and masts, scattered
> among the wild jagged rocks,
> is of an apparent translucence
> like the small old buildings with an emerald moss
> growing on their shoreward walls.

The *s* sounds sustain the single image of silver, and yet ultimately the eye processes the different values associated with this colour as reflected in sea and on land, a difference between opacity and translucency, or 'apparent' translucency. The odd use of 'apparent' here ensures that we don't establish a simple dichotomy between land and sea as sometimes happens in criticism of this complex poem in which nothing, especially the acquisition of knowledge, is easy.

Bishop's delight in colour, its many shades, and shadow—in the same poem she'll speak of 'bluish' Christmas trees 'associating with their shadows'—invites an amateur's game of singling out favourite passages without pressing the heavy pedal of symbolism. We might regard the fish in 'The Fish' as a painter's paradise, and also a reader's. It introduces almost every colour in the palette:

several browns, 'fine rosettes of lime', 'tiny white sea-lice', 'rags of green weed', 'dramatic reds and blacks | of his shiny entrails, | and the pink swim-bladder | like a big peony'—all summed up in the exclamation to colour at the poem's end: 'rainbow, rainbow, rainbow! | And I let the fish go.' As well she might; there's little left to describe in this most Dutch of her poems, a near still-life featuring even a microscopic close-up of the fish's glassy and 'yellowed' eye.

For sheer lightness of touch with colour, we might turn in another direction, to the end of 'A Cold Spring'. 'The smallest moths, like Chinese fans | flatten themselves, silver and silver-gilt | over pale yellow, orange, or gray', a passage followed by a bit of Marvellian wit (sparked by a reminiscence of 'The Mower to the Glow-worms'):

> Now, from the thick grass, the fireflies
> begin to rise:
> up, then down, then up again:
> lit on the ascending flight,
> drifting simultaneously to the same height,
> —exactly like the bubbles in champagne.

Bishop's similes, like this one, are often unlikely likes, and yet also perfectly chosen for the occasion, here yoking together the natural and the social world in this complimentary landscape poem written to her friend Jane Dewey.

As for weightiness of sight and sound, matching the 'silver' of 'At the Fishhouses', here is a golden moment from 'Santarém', again important for firmly anchoring the poem in a specific time and place:

> The street was deep in dark-gold river sand
> damp from the ritual afternoon rain,
> and teams of zebus plodded, gentle, proud,

and *blue*, with down-curved horns and hanging ears,
pulling carts with solid wheels.
The zebus' hooves, the people's feet
waded in golden sand,
dampered by golden sand,
so that almost the only sounds
were creaks and *shush, shush, shush*.

Clearly, this isn't the work of a painter only, but the painter in conjunction with the poet, attentive to sight, sound, and, above all, to the slow movement of feet, poetry's terrain. Note the careful use of pauses and repetition of phrases capturing a sense of the street's quiet activity, animal and human alike, working and walking in relative harmony. Against this background of gold, what also stands out in italics is the colour blue to mark the species of a particular kind of zebus. It is both a decorative colour and a darkening blue speck in the mind's eye that will also be picked up later in the poem in the 'occasional blue eyes' of families from the American South, who, after the Civil War, came to live here where 'they could still own slaves'. The colour reappears then, at the end, in the reference to 'the blue pharmacy', which serves as a medicinal gallery of sorts, where the pharmacist hangs 'an empty wasps' nest from a shelf: | small, exquisite, clean matte white, | and hard as stucco'—like a Calder mobile frozen in space.

The pollinating white page

On a more sophisticated, reflective level, if a Bishop painting could be about the size of a sheet of paper for a poem, then the notion of the white page as a receptive space for colour hints at the related idea of the plenitude of surfaces in Bishop's poems: flat planes such as mirrors, books, maps, and water on which objects appear. One of her most brilliant early poems, 'possibly her masterpiece' writes John Ashbery, 'Over 2,000 Illustrations and a Complete Concordance' invites the reader on an extensive visual pilgrimage to the largely ancient world as found in a popular household Bible Bishop would have known. Largely ancient, because in following out 'God's spreading fingerprint', Bishop travels across time as well as space, as we enter the eye of a poet no longer bound to

> a page made up
> of several scenes arranged in cattycornered rectangles
> or circles set on stippled gray,
> granted a grim lunette,
> caught in the toils of an initial letter....

But Bishop also never quite forgets the medium of the book, as she reminds us near the end: 'Everything only connected by "and" and "and"', in the manner, that is, of someone turning the pages looking for connections rather than rising to some higher synthesis of meaning or interpretation as these biblical 'ands' might imply. In the process of looking, though, she lays the foundation for one of her richest endings:

> Open the book. (The gilt rubs off the edges
> of the pages and pollinates the fingertips.)
> Open the heavy book. Why couldn't we have seen
> this old Nativity while we were at it?
> —the dark ajar, the rocks breaking with light,
> an undisturbed, unbreathing flame,
> colorless, sparkless, freely fed on straw,
> and, lulled within, a family with pets,
> —and looked and looked our infant sight away.

The properties Bishop most admires in poetry are all brilliantly compounded here: spontaneity ('Open the book'), accuracy ('the gilt rubs off the edges'), and mystery, beginning with the pollinated fingertips somehow giving rise (through the pun on 'guilt' being rubbed off?) to the second injunction to 'Open the heavy book'. Mystery, with a capital M, then carries on in the company of spontaneity and accuracy all the way through the wished-for visionary glimpse of the holy family—'a family with pets'—to the final line.

Ashbery again: 'After twenty years…I am unable to exhaust the meaning and mysteries of its concluding line.' Does it mean something like 'looked and looked' until I had grown up? Or 'looked and looked' until saturated with what I saw? Or is it an expression of pure silent happiness, until such looking gave way, perforce, to speaking? And is the 'we' us, the reader and speaker, glimpsing askew, through 'the dark ajar', a new world in the present, one opened up on the page not by a door but by dashes? And does the whole scene perhaps represent the purest expression in Bishop of longing for a family?

Surrealism

As a poet of the 20th century Bishop lived through more than one modernist movement in art. We've already touched on Picasso's '*Guernica* picture' in her letter to Moore, thus raising the distant possibility of a cubist element lurking in the multiple perspectives on the roosters in that poem, and sensed her weariness with abstract expressionism. Recent critics have also explored specific affinities with Calder, Schwitters, and Klee, and with the visual poetry of the international avant-garde. But the general artistic movement most often thought to influence Bishop is surrealism, 'characterized by a fascination with the bizarre, the incongruous and the irrational', including the subconscious and dreams. Few critics agree over the exact nature of the influence, which is hardly surprising given the multiple strands of surrealism that quickly emerged in the 1920s and 1930s in the wake of André Breton's 1924 manifesto. Bishop herself famously backtracked regarding the place of surrealism (and Max Ernst in particular) in her poetry in a worried letter to her publisher at Houghton Mifflin—'I have disliked all of his painting intensely and am not a surrealist'—only to reassess surrealism in a different, more agreeable, if still somewhat mysterious, light in what has come to be known as her 'Darwin' letter.

Written in 1964 to Anne Stevenson, who was writing a
book—the first book—on the author, Bishop proposed a
not-altogether-transparent version of surrealism, one that,
contra Breton, carefully resists the irrational as the source
of inspiration in art:

> Dreams, works of art (some), glimpses of the always-more-successful
> surrealism of everyday life, unexpected moments of empathy
> (is it?), catch a peripheral vision of whatever it is one can never
> really see full-face but that seems enormously important. I can't
> believe we are wholly irrational—and I do admire Darwin! But
> reading Darwin, one admires the beautiful solid case being built up
> out of his endless heroic *observations*, almost unconscious or
> automatic—and then comes a sudden relaxation, a forgetful phrase,
> and one *feels* the strangeness of his undertaking, sees the lonely
> young man, his eyes fixed on facts and minute details, sinking or
> sliding giddily off into the unknown. What one seems to want in art,
> in experiencing it, is the same thing that is necessary for its
> creation, a self-forgetful, perfectly useless concentration.
>
> (In this sense it is always 'escape', don't you think?)

The passage is complex enough to have merited an entire scholarly
book, but a few points are worth making here: that Bishop's
poetry, especially the early poems, reveal a fascination for the
bizarre, the strange, and often involve sleep, dreams, and the
unconscious. 'The Weed' is frequently singled out in this regard,
following an acknowledged debt to Max Ernst's *Histoire naturelle*.
But Bishop conceives these moments as rationally processed,
detail by detail, with the kind of heroic diligence she admired in
Darwin. Coincidental with, or underlying this belief, is an
understanding that the 'surrealism of everyday life' is always more
successful (than passively reiterating dreams, for instance) since it
includes 'unexpected moments of empathy', moments more fully
registered because seen out of the corner of one's eye, perhaps like
the late appearance of the armadillo, or the 'dark ajar' that admits
an 'undisturbed, unbreathing flame' associated with the nativity.

And a third point, ripe for confusion, is the often-quoted phrase 'a self-forgetful, perfectly useless concentration'. Bishop likens it to 'escape' (but not to escapism), an escape, that is, from the 'self' in the process of achieving objectivity, and 'useless' in the sense of not having overt designs on an audience wanting to 'experience' a work of art. One can understand, in a flash, why confessional poetry would be anathema to Bishop, and political poetry something she couldn't write, or, if she tried her hand at it, why it wasn't published.

One way to think of surrealism in Bishop is less as a specific influence and more a general attribute, a way of describing an effect present in the poetry quite different from the Dutch emphasis on realism, and thus an important ingredient in the balance her poems so often achieve. Surrealism doesn't explain how a poem gets written. Darwin, Morris Croll, and the writings of other poets are better guides to this process; but it does point to the 'strangeness' we often encounter in her poetry, a sense of 'strangeness' equally, if differently, present in her early as well as late poetry, in 'The Man-Moth' as well as 'The Moose'. And that 'strangeness' is something she and we also associate with empathy. As she says with regard to the sudden late appearance of the moose in 'The Moose', a poem rich with hallucinations, 'Why, why do we feel | (we all feel) this sweet | sensation of joy?' The comparable moment in 'The Man-Moth' is less obviously marked but still there in the mysterious image of the 'one tear, his only possession' that, 'if you watch, he'll hand it over'. It is the kind of 'strangeness' or mystery an earlier culture would have associated with a religious epiphany, a topic that Bishop will also see out of the corner of her eye in 'Twelfth Morning; or What you Will'.

The analogies to the arts are many and complex in Bishop—and nothing has yet been said about her affinities with Joseph Cornell, the American sculptor most famous for his unusual boxes and almost her exact contemporary (1903–73). In *Geography III*, Bishop dedicated 'Objects & Apparitions' to Cornell, her translation (and the only translation she ever published in one of her collections), of a poem by the Mexican poet Octavio Paz, whom she met while teaching at Harvard. It is possible to see their twin interests in realism and surrealism reflected in the poem's title, but the parallels between artist and poet also stem from a common belief that minimal objects could be conveyers of history, a shared aesthetics of much in little, as the opening stanza suggests:

> Hexahedrons of wood and glass,
> scarcely bigger than a shoebox,
> with room in them for night and all its lights.

Size and value

Apart from wrestling on and off with surrealism, Bishop's writings have little to say about large movements and much to say about individual artists and their work, usually in the form of personal opinions that serve as an index of her taste. A brief, four-paragraph gallery note for a show in 1967 by a former student, Wesley Wehr, is one of her most concise and far-reaching:

> It is a great relief to see a small work of art these days. The Chinese unrolled their precious scroll-paintings to show their friends, bit by bit; the Persians passed their miniatures about from hand to hand; many of Klee's or Bissier's paintings are hand-size. Why shouldn't we, so generally addicted to the gigantic, at last have some small works of art, some short poems, short pieces of music (Mr. Wehr was originally a composer, and I think I detect the influence of Webern on his painting), some intimate, low-voiced, and delicate things in our mostly huge and roaring, glaring world? But in spite of their size, no one could say that these pictures are 'small-scale'.

This centrally placed statement illuminates almost every aspect of Bishop's art. It rises to the level of vintage Bishop in part because of the paragraphs that frame it. The first begins, offering eye-witness testimony of the artist's magic: 'I have seen Mr. Wehr open his battered brief-case (with the broken zipper) at a table in a crowded, steamy coffee-shop, and deal out his latest paintings, carefully encased in plastic until they are framed, like a set of magic playing cards.' The third paragraph begins on a note of hearsay: 'Mr. Wehr works at night, I was told, with his waxes and pigments, while his cat rolls crayons about on the floor.' But we don't doubt its accuracy any more than we question her description of his 'battered brief-case' and the magic it contains. Wehr, in his self-forgetful concentration, and his works are at the forefront of Bishop's thoughts as her final sentence makes clear: 'Who does not feel a sense of release, of calm and quiet, in looking at these little pieces of our vast and ancient world that one can actually hold in the palm of one's hand?' Yes, the hand again, this time receiving what was earlier only shown to his audience. We recall its multiple ramifications: the hand that holds pen and brush; that shows works of art to a select few, like a card dealer, and passes them down from generation to generation; that serves as a measure of the ideal size of a work of art, turning its gracious holder into a momentary god, self-forgetful.

The views in the gallery note not only describe beliefs central to Bishop; they illuminate, in different ways, the pair of poems Bishop wrote about paintings, one near the beginning of her career, 'Large Bad Picture', and one near the end and simply called 'Poem'. The two are Bishop's only 'ekphrastic' poems, in the narrow sense often employed in literary criticism to refer to a poem about an artwork, usually a painting. The doors open wider if we use 'ekphrasis' in the original classical sense of any verbal description of something seen (think 'Cape Breton'), and wider still if used in the 'notional' sense of a specific work of art the poet has not necessarily seen but imagined, like the Portuguese tapestries in 'Brazil, January 1, 1502'. What these two ekphrastic poems have in common is the unusual fact that both paintings were done by the same family artist, her great-uncle George Hutchinson.

'Poem' is clearly the better of the two poems. One would say 'greater' but that seems a violation of the aesthetics terms Bishop so evidently favours. It contains a lifetime of thinking about art and practising it on the page, and it possesses a life well beyond her own work in enunciating a particular aesthetic of 'looking' that has lit up the work of some of her followers. So it is especially good to have an eminent poet like Don Paterson single out 'Large Bad Picture' as being 'one of the five poems I wish I had written'. Paterson's reasons are compelling. They stem largely from the emphasis he places on Bishop's generosity. The poem's title, he suggests, might lead us to think that what follows will be a sophisticated airing at the expense of the painting, but that is not what emerges. Instead we have, in its use of a simple ballad form, a poet looking across not down at the painting and finding only points of interest to describe and a few questions to raise. These begin with the possibility that the painting represents a time of freedom for the artist before exchanging hats for the more humdrum life of a schoolteacher (a worry Bishop also shared, and perhaps made up for the occasion since Hutchinson never became a schoolteacher):

> Remembering the Strait of Belle Isle or
> some northerly harbor of Labrador,
> before he became a schoolteacher
> a great-uncle painted a big picture.

Bishop then proceeds to describe the picture, and in the process of doing so, she enters into its imaginative life and the painter's technique in ways that are only slightly remarkable compared to what will follow in 'Poem'. High above the 'small black ships',

> over the tall cliffs'
> semi-translucent ranks,
> are scribbled hundreds of fine black birds
> hanging in *n*'s in banks.

One can hear their crying, crying,
the only sound there is
except for occasional sighing
as a large aquatic animal breathes.

Slightly remarkable perhaps but still worth remarking on: there exists a funny exchange between Bishop and her *New Yorker* editors that illuminates much in this poem, and in Bishop. 'Large Bad Picture' was one of her first poems published by the magazine; in fact, it had been rejected earlier, before *North & South* had received the Houghton Mifflin prize that led to the book's publication. Bishop was on a short leash. One problem the poem posed in being published in *The New Yorker* was simply practical: how to represent the *'n's* on the page, 'in caps or lower case', with the editor, Katharine White, remarking: 'I think in New Yorker type that our capital N looks more like the n's most fine black birds make.' Bishop's response is a model of patient industry and precision: 'after looking at all the *n's* in New Yorker type I still think that the lower case n is best, like this'; and she offers a few handwritten examples. 'That is why I said "scribbled". No printed n looks *like* that, but I still think that the lower case one gives the idea best without any attempt at representation.' In other words, this 'n' is what the painter's marks for birds look like. *Hand*-written *'n's*, as Bishop shows her editor, are closer to the truth, and indeed, her written samples do look more like the birds flying in the painting than stilted caps would ever allow. Bishop's hand and eye won the day.

A second, equally curious problem occurs with Bishop's reference to the 'large aquatic animal'. One of the editors, she's told, 'hopes you can name the animal—says he didn't realize there were large aquatic animals on the northern coasts'. To which Bishop responds, again a model of patience: 'I am trying to describe a picture and the sounds are imaginary, just for effect. There are no animals in it—although if there were they might perfectly well be something inappropriate'. Bishop's defence is not just of the poet's imagination; her sympathies are with the painter, who might just as easily have made something up 'for effect'. But he didn't, so she did, crossing over into his territory and seeing the world from his (imagined) point of view. Yes, 'Large Bad Picture' might be large and bad. One category often implies the other in Bishop's lexicon. But the painting still invites curiosity and humour, particularly in the image of the 'small red sun [that] goes rolling, rolling', and speculation as to what the ships are doing in the harbour in the first place. Her last thought: 'It would be hard to say what brought them there, | Commerce or Contemplation'. An apparent throwaway, and yet it sticks in the memory, aided by alliteration, and because these apparent opposites contain so much, like Milton's 'L'Allegro' and 'Il Penseroso'.

Twenty-five years later these lines still seem in Bishop's head. We're familiar with Bishop's compositional habits of letting scenes and phrases lie fallow for many years, then eventually turning them into masterpieces—'Crusoe in England', 'The Moose', and 'Santarém' spring to mind. 'Poem', by contrast, is perhaps unique in being a deliberate rewriting of an already finished poem. (I can't help thinking an unspoken link exists between her two ekphrastic poems through Auden's 'Musée des Beaux Arts', which also concludes with the image of ships sailing 'calmly on' and begins, as does Bishop's 'Poem', with a casual use of 'About'.) Not that Bishop didn't get it right for that early poem at that time, but there had been much growth on many fronts since then, including, as 'Poem' vividly demonstrates, how to look with increasing depth at a small painting, and in the process of looking and thinking, to establish value, not just the value of the painting but of the poem as well and its underlying poetics.

'Poem' deserves a chapter of its own rather than a few concluding paragraphs, but in important ways the poem explains its thinking so fully and carefully that its large points about the intertwining of art and life can hardly be missed. Its greatness (its persuasiveness, rather) is a matter of many small effects coming together. Here the effects include Bishop's mastery of detail, intensified by the sheer smallness of the painting; her keen response to the artist's technique, going well beyond the obvious 'n's of 'Large Bad Picture'; her brilliant command of the trope of self-correction, or 'metanoia', as a means of spelling out a mind constantly opening up to the occasion, even to the point of epiphany ('Heavens, I recognize the place, I know it!); her decision to withhold the artist's biography until *after* his work has been examined, its provenance understood as 'a minor family relic', a biography sketched out through the intimate revelation in italics of a network of family connections by an unnamed speaker, who is also given to self-correction ('Your Uncle George, no, mine, my Uncle George | he'd be your great-uncle'); and verse that is metrically varied, subtly expressive, and confident every step of the way.

This is a painting, in other words, that inspires contemplation of the most concentrated order, hers, ours. On the crucial topic of empathy for another, an artist she never, in fact, met, she writes,

> I never knew him. We both knew this place,
> apparently, this literal small backwater,
> looked at it long enough to memorize it,
> our years apart. How strange. And it's still loved,
> or its memory is (it must have changed a lot).
> Our visions coincided—'visions' is
> too serious a word—our looks, two looks:
> art 'copying from life' and life itself,
> life and the memory of it so compressed
> they've turned into each other. Which is which?

Bishop's diminution of the visionary moment is classic, as is her own self-correction, dividing 'our looks' into 'two looks', responsive to both similarity and difference, his looks and hers. Putting quotation marks around the familiar view of art 'copying from life' recognizes a cliché but also draws attention to the fact that both artist and poet are doing the same thing, but in different ways. He copies nature with a brush, she copies his art with a pen, but with an eye to nature as she comes to remember it, with memory becoming the life of her own poem, a memory that grows to include him, in a space made exquisite by its size, of a place made precious by a sense of its passing.

> Life and the memory of it cramped,
> dim, on a piece of Bristol board,
> dim, but how live, how touching in detail
> —the little that we get for free,
> the little of our earthly trust. Not much.
> About the size of our abidance
> along with theirs: the munching cows,
> the iris, crisp and shivering, the water
> still standing from spring freshets,
> the yet-to-be dismantled elms, the geese.

The final lines are among Bishop's most moving. Poetry does what painting can't: embody change, here with religious intonations and reverberations. Bishop's recapitulation of elements in the landscape is the poem's last 'metanoia'. The temporal pulse of the poem increases in the mounting use of the present participle, only to become suddenly retrospective, or rather quietly prophetic, in its inclusion of the 'yet-to-be dismantled elms', the hyphens suggesting their already precarious state. Not much—the sentence stops in mid-air, or rather continues indefinitely, like geese flying—but it is enough to admit a sidelong, ecological glance into the future. 'Poem' is older and wiser than 'Large Bad Picture', a touch sadder in what it says about art, 'the little we get for free', and yet modestly triumphant: 'how touching in detail'. The balance is exquisite. When Bishop sent it to a grateful Howard Moss at *The New Yorker*, she simply remarked: 'Here's an old-fashioned umpty-umpty nostalgic poem that perhaps you'll be able to use.' His response, after having read it: 'I wish I could read a poem like that every day for the rest of my life.'

7. Rollie McKenna, 'Elizabeth Bishop', *c.*1961, in Loren MacIver's studio, Greenwich Village.

Chapter 5
Love known

The most recent Bishop biography by Thomas Travisano bears the curious title *Love Unknown: The Life and Worlds of Elizabeth Bishop*. The first part of the title forms an allusion to a favourite poem of hers by George Herbert, 'Love Unknown'. But how the title applies to Bishop's life or to her worlds is less clear and never directly addressed. Can it be that love was unknown to her (Figure 7)?

This seems hardly likely, but it raises an important question sounded early on in her career when her poetry was sometimes criticized for its 'coldness and precision'. Bishop was perplexed and upset by these descriptions, and on one occasion she countered by writing to a friend, 'at least I don't *feel* as if I wrote that way'. Presumably, Bishop didn't *feel* 'that way' because she expended considerable passion (and intelligence) in the act of writing, and because, like most people, Bishop spent much time thinking about love. Love was also something she clearly experienced in her life on more than one occasion, and sometimes for long stretches with one person, in the cases of Lota de Macedo Soares and Alice Methfessel.

How the question of love figures in her poetry is a complex story that forms the subject of this chapter. A long view of the topic tells us that, despite her early admiration of Elizabethan verse, Bishop was not a great love poet in the tradition of Shakespeare and Donne, in whom love is the motivating impulse of poem after poem—154 of them in the case of Shakespeare's Sonnets. Love does not rise to the declamatory heights of Shakespeare's famous 'marriage sonnet' 116 ('Let me not to the marriage of true minds, | Admit impediments'), or of any number of Donne poems that, using direct address, situate the lover and the beloved at the centre of the universe, as in 'The Sun Rising' or 'The Canonization'. But a more nuanced, less lofty view underscores love's continuing presence as a subject in her verse. Think of the hapless hermit from *North & South* shooting off his gun in sexual frustration in 'Chemin de fer' or, from the same volume, the mysterious homage to love in 'Late Air', with not one but five 'Phoenixes | burning quietly'. Or, much later, recall the simple, heart-breaking lines at the end of 'Crusoe in England' in *Geography III*: '—And Friday, my dear Friday, died of measles | Seventeen years ago come March'. In this regard, Bishop is not so much a great love poet as a great poet who wrote about love from many angles: love between people, love for animals and plants, love for the environment, different kinds of love sometimes bound together in a single setting, as in 'Song for the Rainy Season'—and deplored when absent, as in 'Pink Dog'. We have already sensed as much in the tenderness expressed in 'The Armadillo', and also the accompanying outrage.

Closets, and more closets

The poet Richard Howard offers a light-hearted entry into our topic. The date is sometime in the mid-1970s, when the first wave of the women's liberation movement was in full swing.

> Adrienne Rich had been to see Elizabeth in Boston and had attempted to persuade her to be more forthcoming about her sexual orientation. Elizabeth did not regard the enterprise with favour. After Adrienne's visit, I remember her describing her new domesticities at Lewis Wharf. 'You know what I want, Richard? I want closets, closets, and more closets! And she laughed.

Rich was 18 years younger than Bishop, but, along with temperamental differences, the two seemed to belong to entirely different generations when it came to the public expression of sexual attitudes. As the joke about closets suggests, Bishop was always more comfortable thinking about love as a private matter, an attitude that seems only in part owing to historical circumstance. In the 1930s, when Bishop began writing poetry seriously, the available models of women poets voicing female desire (Elizabeth Barrett Browning, say, or Edna St Vincent Millay) were not poets who instinctively attracted her, or if they did, such as Dickinson, were too outspoken about passion; and though Bishop became more open to expressions of love in her own work, she always maintained a careful distance between what might be said in private and what could or should appear in her published writings.

As a consequence, her most forthright, intimate declarations of amorous or erotic love remained closeted, locked in manuscript during her lifetime, coming to light only after her death. The inspired aubade 'It is marvellous to wake up together', written about her relationship with either Louise Crane or Marjorie Stevens, dates back to the late 1930s or early 1940s, although it is one of the most finished of her unpublished poems, as is another aubade, 'Breakfast Song' ('My love, my saving grace'), written in the 1970s, presumably with Alice Methfessel in mind. Likewise, her most explicitly homoerotic poem, '*Vague Poem* (vaguely love poem)', with its sensuous evocation of roses à la Gertrude Stein as a metaphor for the most intimate aspects of the female body, did not appear in print until 2000.

One exception, and it is only a partial exception since it is not a love poem per se, is the wittily transgressive poem 'Exchanging Hats'. The poem is a funny riff on two 'unfunny uncles' and two 'Anandrous aunts' who like to cross-dress. (A funny uncle is code for a gay one; anandrous, a botanical term, means without a stamen, or husbandless.) It appeared in print in April 1956, in

New World Writing, and in 1993 was given a public reading by James Merrill, easily found today on YouTube with a Merrill impersonator comically performing the swift exchange of 'headgear'. But Bishop never included the poem among her published collections of verse. Whether she didn't want to offend her relatives or simply thought the poem too revealing—'we share your slight transvestite twist | in spite of our embarrassment'—or tonally out of sync with the other poems in, say, the 'Elsewhere' section of *Questions of Travel*, it nonetheless underscores a playful side involving the gender-bending complexities of 'Costumes and custom' occasionally hinted at in the poetry.

I have in mind here Bishop's early re-fashioning of Tennyson's 'The Lady of Shalott' into 'The Gentleman of Shalott'. 'A little fey, even precious', the gentleman plays a jaunty counter-tenor in dimeter verse, in which 'half is enough', to Tennyson's melancholic basso-continuo describing the lady's descent into death. Even more to the point is the comic moment in 'Arrival at Santos', in which the poet describes 'myself and a fellow passenger named Miss Breen', climbing backwards down a ladder,

> descending into the midst of twenty-six freighters
> waiting to be loaded with green coffee beans.
> Please, boy, do be more careful with that boat hook!
> Watch out! Oh! It has caught Miss Breen's
>
> skirt! There! Miss Breen is about seventy,
> a retired police lieutenant, six feet tall,
> with beautiful bright blue eyes and a kind expression.
> Her home, when she is at home, is in Glens Fall
>
> s, New York. There. We are settled.

Rarely has an enjambment across a stanza been handled more playfully than the one involving Miss Breen's 'skirt!' Another country, other customs, and a costume we almost see through—'There!'—leaving just a trace of *eros* on the page in the eye beholding the 'beautiful bright blue eyes and a kind expression' and in the startling textual slippage involving the subsequent missing 's' in 'Glens Fall' (for Glens Falls, New York) that reappears on its own at the beginning of the next stanza in the strange, slippery line, 's, New York. There. We are settled.' Miss Breen and Miss Bishop have landed, free of any mishap, in their usual dress, but for a moment there is a frisson of befuddlement, a little slippage on the part of the speaker-poet. In such moments, we recall that Bishop's two favourite Shakespeare plays were *As You Like It* and *Twelfth Night*, with their cross-dressing heroines, and that costumes could carry an erotic touch in Bishop, as some readers find in her 'Invitation to Miss Marianne Moore'.

'Queer cupids'

Bishop's instinctive preference for 'closets, closets, and more closets' no doubt influenced the shaping of her love poetry. But so did a number of other features, including her age and developing poetics as well as her keen sense of place, place being understood both in a geographical and generic sense, as literary topoi, and her belief, as always, that one should never repeat. Her earliest poems about love are often 'queer cupids' ('Love Lies Sleeping') of a sort, wrapped in the language of another (Felicia Hemans's in 'Casabianca', Tennyson's in 'The Gentleman of Shalott'), or serving as an occasion for cruising the city in 'Love Lies Sleeping', the only poem of hers with love in the title and where the striking phrase 'queer cupids' appears. It is the hermit, not Bishop, who cries 'Love should be put in action', at least not the Bishop of *North & South*. She everywhere prefers to shadow-box with the topic and its tropes: sleeping with an unspecified other, a 'we', either on the ceiling or standing up, in the pair of poems using those fanciful locations in their titles, or forming, *sotto voce*, the amatory understory in 'Roosters'. She winsomely but coyly rewrites the

Phoenix myth in 'Late Airs' as 'Five remote red lights | keep their nests there; Phoenixes | burning quietly, where the dew cannot climb.'

These and other early poems invite but ultimately resist amatory decoding. Surely we can read those 'five remote red lights' symbolically and 'their nests' sexually. Or can we? More often than not, sexuality in this volume is in the eye of the beholder, including the reader. The gendering of pronouns goes unidentified, a cover Bishop may have learned from Auden in his early poems, whose 'sexual courage' she later praised, along with his 'technically dazzling poetry'. Occasionally, however, a poem will seem emotionally overcharged by insinuating a back story that it skilfully refuses to deliver. The end of 'Quai d'Orléans', an emblem poem of dazzling virtuosity in its use of metre, image, and rhyme, concludes by suddenly introducing a 'we' into the poem. Usually, the 'we' in early Bishop is never or barely developed (see the opening lines of 'Anaphora'), but in this case the pronoun marks the shift in the poem's focus, and both speaker and implied listener—the projected other—assume a sense of presence:

> We stand as still as stones to watch
>   the leaves and ripples
> while light and nervous water hold
>   their interview.
> 'If what we see could forget us half as easily',
>   I want to tell you,
> 'as it does itself—but for life we'll not be rid
>   Of the leaves' fossils'.

The first four lines hardly need glossing; the water serves to reflect the nervous conversation about to occur, as the two people stand on the solid stone footing of the quay. The final four lines, however, almost exceed our attempt to fathom what is exactly being said, or rather not being said. To read the poem from the beginning is to know that leaves can readily be forgotten in the wake of a barge, 'real leaves', in fact, as Bishop twice declares, but not the past as inscribed in the memory of the living. Those fossils continue on. The poem, among the most moving in this first collection, is often read in light of the traumatic injury Bishop's friend Margaret Miller—to whom the poem is dedicated—suffered in a car accident in France, in which Bishop was present. But there is more to their relationship than that. The interrupted thought, the halting syntax, the splintering of 'we' into 'I' and 'you', tell us this much and also how much more is left unsaid. This is not so much Bishop being reticent; reticence, rather, is the cry of the poem's occasion.

The tumult in the heart

Quiet as it is, 'Quai' is something of a breakthrough poem in breaking the line and giving voice to private utterance. As a means to suggest an emotion exceeding its boundaries, it looks ahead to Bishop's most celebrated love poem, 'One Art', and its famous last stanza. More immediately, however, it points to the brief suite of 'passionately personal' love poems in *A Cold Spring* appearing under the simple banner of 'Four Poems'. Each is given its own subtitle addressing different aspects or moments of love: 'I | Conversation'; 'II | Rain Towards Morning'; 'III | While Someone Telephones', and 'IV | O Breath'. Their fragmentary quality helps to create a level of urgency not found elsewhere in a volume that otherwise shows Bishop warming to the topic of love. Each feels quickly struck, overcharged with emotion, suggesting a poet chafing at the amatory constraints of her first volume. As she wrote to her friends, U.T. and Joseph Summers, 'The "Four Poems" are certainly fragmentary & probably too much so, but I thought that together they made a sort of emotional sequence (maybe not) a la [Tennyson's] *Maude*, with the story left out.' Tennyson, again, but now to plumb, not to ironize, feeling.

'Sequence' is probably too strong a term, as Bishop suggests, but it's possible to glimpse a beginning in 'Conversation' in the opening reference to 'the tumult in the heart', although whether she is speaking to an imaginary other or to her poetic self is left up in the air. 'Rain Towards Morning' goes on to describe a sudden change in (outer and/or inner) weather that issues in a moment of pre-dawn intimacy in an 'unexpected kiss'. 'While Someone Telephones' returns to the problem of a distracted conversation, but this time with a great weight placed on the truncated eighth line, *'nothing. And wait'*, with 'wait' being the word on which this jagged-lined sonnet turns in hope of 'the heart's release'. The concluding poem, 'O Breath', then serves as a final abject reckoning of the lover to the beloved.

'All poetry is experimental poetry,' wrote Wallace Stevens in *Adagia*, but some poems seem more wilfully experimental than others, and so it is with 'Four Poems'. (The writing of them coincided with a period of Bishop's greatest self-doubt as a poet.) The most interesting, in this regard, is 'O Breath', a title that has suggested to some a biographical connection to Bishop's lifelong battle with asthma. Of greater literary interest is the presence of the space within each line, in conjunction with the marked use of alliteration, as a reminder of the 'strong-stress' metre and caesura of Anglo-Saxon poetry, where breath is especially needed in the service of speaking the line:

> Beneath that loved   and celebrated breast
> silent, bored really   blindly veined,
> grieves, maybe   lives and lets
> live…

If alliteration marks out 'Beneath' and 'breast' for special attention in these first lines, then the space within the line, the gap between the phrases (signalling a space between the lovers?), adds a further level of emotional stress in a poem about love—that of an utterance struggling to be spoken. The heart heaves almost with every word. And with each heave, the halting Anglo-Saxon cadence also has the effect of turning the poem in a strange but, to my ear, emphatically Shakespearian direction, not only because its 15 lines are of near sonnet length or because the Sonnets encourage or endorse a view of same-sex love, but because the portrait of the lovers here, in conjunction with the bitter word-play (the pun on 'blindly veined' with its suggestion of vanity, for instance, or the equivocation involving 'equivocal' and 'equivalents', and 'breath' and 'breast'), underscores the painful hierarchical distance often found in the Sonnets and the abject position the lover is placed in, in relation to the beloved. In this case 'Beneath' that 'celebrated breast'—'celebrated' in what sense, we wonder, and by whom?—the lover is further tortured by 'the thin flying   of nine black hairs | four around one   five the other nipple, | flying almost intolerably   on your own breath'. Bishop's letters are filled with self-recriminations and apologies (as are Shakespeare's Sonnets), but rarely does she strike so exacting a note of emotional undoing in her poetry as in the end of 'O Breath', right down, one feels, to the last word-mincing distinction between 'within   if never with':

Equivocal, but what we have in common's   bound to be there,
whatever we must own   equivalents for,
something that maybe I   could bargain with
and make a separate peace   beneath
within   if never with.

The mantra at the end of 'The Bight', 'awful but cheerful', doesn't work here. And so it is, in the next poem, we see Bishop repairing to the well-lit, if still fraught, social world of the familiar verse epistle in 'Letter to N.Y.', dedicated to Louise Crane, with its joke about sowing wheat, not oats. It comes immediately after 'Four Poems', at least in the order as presented in *The Complete Poems* (1969). In the original publication of *A Cold Spring* in 1955, 'Four Poems' was followed by 'Argument', another lovers' quarrel poem, although less intense. But by 1969, the more public Bishop perhaps thought the reader needed a bit more breathing room after the four poems she once called 'a sketch for an acute, neurotic, "modern" drama'.

Still explosions

Bishop closed *A Cold Spring* on more than a cheerful note. 'The Shampoo', called 'Gray Hairs' in an earlier draft, is a true-blue love poem, as almost everyone who has ever encountered it has realized, even perhaps Katharine White, Bishop's editor at *The New Yorker*, when she rejected it. (The poem eventually appeared in *The New Republic* in 1955.) Bishop reported to her friend Pearl Kazin that White professed she 'couldn't understand' it. 'The Shampoo' certainly has some of the complexity of a 17th-century metaphysical poem. But its amatory subject matter and situation can hardly be in doubt, leaving us to suspect that the understory of lesbian sexuality surfacing here was too much for the magazine at the time. Although Bishop fiddled a bit with the final construction of *A Cold Spring*—as mentioned in Chapter 3, 'Arrival at Santos', the next to last poem in *A Cold Spring*, later became the introductory poem in *Questions of Travel*—she always left 'The Shampoo' in its place as the final poem in the collection. The poem is, in this regard, quietly triumphant, with *A Cold Spring* ending on a warm note. And once separated from 'Arrival at Santos', the poem assumes a greater sense of universality—a stance already indicated in the macrocosmic imagery that runs through the poem: from the moon to the heavens to shooting stars, images that all reflect on the lovers' circumstances below.

'The Shampoo' begins on an erotically suggestive but slightly perplexing note, especially if our initial reading of the first line is being guided by the poem's title:

> The still explosions on the rocks,
> the lichens, grow
> by spreading, gray, concentric shocks.
> They have arranged
> to meet the rings around the moon, although
> within our memories they have not changed.

Odd to think of lichens exploding; odder still to think of them as still, unmoving, when exploding; more unusual yet, but to the point, is to hear in lichens, 'liken', in a poem rich with similitudes and connections. Lichens do grow by spreading in grey concentric shocks, as do perhaps shocks of hair turning grey, but these changes are not disturbing to this speaker who sees in the image of the circle the kind of unchanging coronal Donne might have glimpsed. (Donne's 'La Corona' was a poem Bishop knew well.)

And the connections continue. The second of the three stanzas reads:

> And since the heavens will attend
> as long on us,
> you've been, dear friend,
> precipitate and pragmatical;
> and look what happens. For Time is
> nothing if not amenable.

The cordial address, 'dear friend', is tactfully reminiscent of the opening address of Herbert's 'Love Unknown', but with the idea of 'unknown' now no longer applying. The immediacy of tender address to another isn't something we've heard before in Bishop. Bishop is speaking to Lota de Macedo Soares, but who would know it on the basis of the poem alone—unless one saw on the facing page in *The Complete Poems* (1969) the name of the person to whom *Questions of Travel* is dedicated? The elegant phrase 'precipitate and pragmatical' is also a revision of the earlier blunt remark, 'demanding and too voluble'. Lota could be both, as well as possess a grey streak in her hair. In the words of one of the poem's most adept critics: 'This is an after-the-fact poem by a coy mistress feeling pushed into something, yet glad to have been pushed.' The final lines tell us, though, that this is not Marvell's 'Coy Mistress'. Time is not a winged chariot but courteously 'amenable'; and so is the poet, who will leisurely arrive at her moment of request.

Direct address, in the company of a refined character description, points to the full presence of the beloved in a manner Bishop had not attempted before, a presence clinched and celebrated in the brilliant Petrarchan stellification of Lota's hair in the final stanza (with 'bright' rightly replacing the earlier 'swift'):

> The shooting stars in your black hair
> in bright formation
> are flocking where,
> so straight, so soon?
> —Come, let me wash it in this big tin basin
> battered and shiny like the moon.

So coy and yet so down to earth, as that last image tells us. There is urgency in the shooting stars, even if we don't quite know where they are flocking; and we also know, by virtue of the poem's title, that permission will be granted (has already been granted) to the initiator of the invitation, who sets off with a dash (for spontaneity) and a comma (for a pause), the single word 'Come', a directive that carries lightly the weight of an entire tradition of *carpe diem* poems in English. (Think Marlowe's 'Come live with me' or Ben Jonson's 'Come my Celia, let us prove | The sports of love.') And in that directive, we might fancy Bishop taking control of those loose black hairs in 'O Breath' that were flying around, intolerably blown about, and weaving them into a love-knot about something as domestically simple and sensual as washing a companion's hair.

Brazil: account books, dream books

Another poet might settle in for a long stay with love poetry in the manner of 'The Shampoo'. (Bishop's letters describing her early days in Brazil with Lota are filled with a sense of rapture over her new arrangement.) But not Bishop, at least not directly. The landscape of her newly adopted country, its rituals, and customs (as in 'The Armadillo'), and its people, especially those on the fringe of society, allowed her geographical imagination greater room for exploration and poetic expression. Maybe, too, Bishop had been spurred to think in this wider direction by Katharine White's stated reason for rejecting the poem: 'I guess the deciding factor was that this sort of small personal poem perhaps doesn't quite fit in *The New Yorker*.' And so, too, by the apparent—and to Bishop puzzling—indifference 'The Shampoo', her most personal poem to date, seems to have received from her friends. It was a troubled coming out.

Even so, Lota is still forcefully present in *Questions of Travel* but as part of a larger, localized landscape. She is the presumed speaker in one of Bishop's longer poems, the dramatic monologue 'Manuelzinho'. Underneath the title we're told in brackets, 'Brazil: a friend of the writer is speaking.' In one of her letters Bishop mentions Lota as the supposed speaker, but we might sense as much because the speaker can be 'demanding' and 'voluble' in places, not features we typically associate with Bishop. Apart from the vast amount of criticism 'Manuelzinho' has generated regarding its colonial politics, what is most interesting about the poem from the perspective of this chapter (and not irrelevant to the politics) is how Bishop has woven and amplified the reserved pronoun dynamics of the earlier love poems into the wider social fabric of daily life in Brazil, represented here between landowner and worker. The poem is a study in the human problem of communication across a wide economic divide, and the cultural and cognitive differences such a division produces. How do these two people connect, if at all? The question is made emphatic by the sheer volume of pronouns in each passage, the most in any Bishop poem. It's also not simply that the speaker is exasperated by Manuelzinho's behaviour and the cultural history and practices underlying it. Every exchange, whether actual or imagined, underscores the speaker's own sense of difference and

95

accompanying sense of instability that comes with this recognition. Humorous, impatient, disbelieving, insulting, apologetic, defensive, confused, the speaker concludes:

> You helpless, foolish man,
> I love you all I can,
> I think. Or do I?
> I take off my hat, unpainted
> and figurative, to you.
> Again I promise to try.

We know who is really feeling helpless and foolish here, and also perhaps loving, as Bishop regards both her subjects from the sidelines. But it is an unusual kind of love, one that exposes, rather than elides, the gaping class differences Bishop is sometime too easily accused of maintaining. In their outrage over the treatment of the poor in Brazil, 'Squatter's Children' and 'Pink Dog' are just around the corner.

The other poem in *Questions of Travel* where we feel Lota's presence is 'Song for the Rainy Season', preceded in this regard by 'Electrical Storm'. Lota is never mentioned by name. In fact, pronouns dwindle to a single 'we', so deeply interfused is the human with the environment, *eros* with habitat, the opening out of one into the other. The idea of sympathy carries some of the weight it once possessed in the Renaissance concept of correspondence as a magnetic force that binds the world together. 'Waterfalls cling'; 'fat frogs…shrilling for love, | clamber and mount'. 'Hidden, oh hidden | in the high fog | the house we live in…' What was a penchant for hermetic privacy in her early poetry is now turned into a visible celebration of hiddenness.

'Song for the Rainy Season' is a love poem of considerable feeling about the Brazilian home Bishop and Machedo Soares shared in 'Petrópolis, Fazenda Samambaia', identified as such at the end of the poem. Lowell remarked that it is 'perfect in the way several poems in *North & South* were perfect', but doesn't say which poems he had in mind. Perhaps 'Jerónimo's House' because of its light touch and domestic subject matter? Bishop responded, rather mysteriously, that 'it seems to me now in rumba rhythm'. Editors have drawn attention to lines about the brook singing 'loud | from a rib cage of giant fern'.

'Song for the Rainy Season' is perfectly pitched in several senses. Lyrical, effortless, flowing, embodying in movement the freedom and openness of the private place it is celebrating, the poem is also highly aware of the fragility of the moment and impending change, of things flowing and flown. This is not a genial *carpe diem* poem in the mode of 'The Shampoo', although it continues the association in Bishop of *eros* with *aqua*, both life-giving forces in Brazil. Rather it is a small hymn to 'maculate' beauty. (How unusual, and right in this context, to strip that term of its virginal associations and set it alongside 'cherish'.) The poem takes into account love's environmental magic, represented in the figure of the magnetic rock, and its mutability in the spectre of climate change. At its most human and warmest in its metonymies, the poem is already looking beyond itself:

> darkened and tarnished
> by the warm touch
> of the warm breath,
> maculate, cherished,
> rejoice! For a later
> era will differ.
> (O difference that kills,
> or intimidates, much
> of all our small shadowy
> life!) Without water
>
> the great rock will stare
> unmagnetized, bare,
> no longer wearing

rainbows or rain,
the forgiving air
and the high fog gone;
the owls will move on
and the several
waterfalls shrivel
in the steady sun.

There is nothing apocalyptic here, just less water and a corresponding loss of fog, love's cover. Small differences that ramify in the figure of the owls' flight is what Bishop's art is always about.

The art of losing

On the far side of 'Song for the Rainy Season' lies Bishop's most famous love poem, the villanelle 'One Art', probably her most frequently anthologized lyric. Published more than 15 years later in *The New Yorker* in 1976, it deepens the elegiac note in 'Song', a note often sounded in the late poems in *Geography III*, all composed, or finished, in the aftermath of Lota's suicide in 1967. 'One Art' also takes the idea of a love song into the realm of the villanelle, with its origins in Italian pastoral folk music. Almost a decade after Lota's death, Bishop wrote to Katharine White, in January 1976, 'I am having a poem in your magazine fairly soon, I think, the one and only villanelle of my life. It is very SAD—it makes everyone weep, so I think it must be rather good, in its awful way, and I hope you will like it.'

It's unusual for Bishop to say much about her poems, let alone toot her own horn just a bit, but given the earlier cool reception of 'The Shampoo' maybe not altogether surprising or unwarranted. Nor that it comes forth well dressed as 'the one and only villanelle of my life', a special poem for a special occasion. The immediate event that inspired the poem, however, was not memories of Lota, even if Bishop's sense of loss and the accompanying guilt filters into the volume (and the poem), but rather her fear of being left by her young lover Alice Methfessel, whom she met at Harvard and on whom, as she aged, she was increasingly dependent.

The villanelle is less formally demanding than the sestina, but Bishop's skill with it, as with the sestina, has helped to assure the form a canonical place among contemporary readers and writers of poetry. Encyclopedias remind us that the villanelle's 19 lines are typically composed of five tercets rhyming *aba*, and a concluding quatrain rhyming *abaa*. Its pattern of repetition is thus a feature of its association with song. The first and third lines of the opening tercet reappear to form the refrain for the subsequent tercets in alternating fashion in the following manner. The first line from stanza 1 reappears at the end of stanzas 2 and 4; the third line reappears at the end of stanzas 3 and 5. Then, in a concluding couplet, these two come together to create the final rhyme of the quatrain.

For all its formal intricacies, 'One Art' was written over a short period. 'It was like writing a letter', Bishop noted, hinting at the fluidity and informality that characterize her poem. Equally remarkable, the villanelle survives in 16 draft versions, allowing new readers and old a fine opportunity to appreciate the care Bishop expended on her creation. Here is the final version as printed in *Geography III*:

> The art of losing isn't hard to master;
> so many things seem filled with the intent
> to be lost that their loss is no disaster.
>
> Lose something every day. Accept the fluster
> of lost door keys, the hour badly spent.
> The art of losing isn't hard to master.
>
> Then practice losing farther, losing faster:
> places, and names, and where it was you meant
> to travel. None of these will bring disaster.

I lost my mother's watch. And look! my last, or
next-to-last, of three loved houses went.
The art of losing isn't hard to master.

I lost two cities, lovely ones. And, vaster,
some realms I owned, two rivers, a continent.
I miss them, but it wasn't a disaster.

—Even losing you (the joking voice, a gesture
I love) I shan't have lied. It's evident
the art of losing's not too hard to master
though it may look like (*Write* it!) like disaster.

One can see at a glance Bishop's habit of arriving obliquely at her
subject, almost in the manner of an afterthought: '—Even losing
you…', as if that loss were not a problem, let alone a 'disaster', one
no greater than losing a set of 'door keys', and therefore an easy
thing to 'master'. Villanelles rise and fall on the memorability of
their two repeating lines. Recall Dylan Thomas's fierce villanelle,
'Do not go gentle into that good night', its famous first line being
answered by the third, 'Rage, rage against the dying of the light'.
Bishop's route is different, quieter, more tonally varied, even a
touch whimsical, placing in opposition two lines with feminine
rhymes no less ('master' and 'disaster'). She also departs from the
usual practice of keeping the third line intact in its subsequent
iterations. She retains just the single rhyme word 'disaster' as the
refrain in stanzas 3 and 5, thus allowing a greater freedom of
expression, as song is tempered into talk—and talk will become an
important marker of the beloved, the parenthetical 'joking voice, a
gesture | I love'.

We love that joking voice in Bishop as well, as she gives away thing
after ever grander thing ('And look!'), even flourishing in the
process a Keatsian gesture in the echo from his sonnet 'Much have
I travelled in the realms of gold'. But as she practises stretching
further, she also prepares for the volta, the emotional collapse of

the quatrain. The drafts show Bishop struggling mightily with this part of the poem, not with the idea of the greater loss of the beloved—that tension is present at the outset—but how to express the conflict without sounding mawkish in the process. An important step was to make the Alice figure less visible (not the same thing as less present) by erasing references to her blue eyes ('eyes of the Azure Aster' in one version), and in turn arriving at 'a gesture | I love', the 'joking voice', a more general evocation of the other that applies equally well to Lota.

The shift in tone is from the sentimental to the more light-hearted. It increases what Lowell called 'your stoical humor', which is carried out further in the speaker's struggle against the poem's logic: that this 'disaster' can be just as easily 'mastered' as the others, an evident lie registered in the grammatical and syntactic contortions that abound in this stanza, including, of course, the claim that she isn't lying. To deepen the sense of emotional struggle, Bishop also makes a single change to the refrain so that it reads 'the art of losing's not *too* hard to master' (my italics), and then enjoins herself to conclude the poem, not by *saying* the word 'disaster' (as existed in the earlier drafts) but to put in parentheses the stronger command, '*Write* it!', offset, however, in the manner of a stutter, through the double use of 'like'. For all its apparent air of nonchalance, this is not a poem easily ended. But 'right' it she does, the author, the writer, true to her one art.

'One Art' is more than the sum of her earlier love poems, but one reason why the poem was written quickly may simply be that Bishop had already navigated much of love's terrain in verse. As with the elegiac turn to loss in 'Song for the Rainy Season', we can see vestiges of some of her previous ventures re-turned here: in the choice of the juxtaposed rhymes, arrived at early in the process of composition, the difference between the element of mastery achieved in 'The Shampoo' and the sense of disaster or disintegration—psychic, emotional, and visual—as recorded in 'O Breath'. If love called her to the things of the world in 'Love Lies Sleeping', things here are readily, if regretfully, renounced as part of the practice, or exercise, for facing the ultimate departure of love itself. So, too, the closing quatrain, in refusing to say what it so evidently wants to say, is reminiscent of the disruption at the end of 'Quai d'Orléans'. And, finally, the elusive, often absent 'you' in Bishop's love poetry receives its full weight here in the poem's final turn: the reference to '—Even losing you'.

'Everyone is moved to tears by it; it certainly is the height of spontaneity, and yet it is so mysterious they are still arguing as to whether it's his own button or his daughter's button.' Bishop is speaking about the end of *King Lear*, but we might also be thinking about the end of 'One Art', 'the joking voice, a gesture | I love', wrapped inside a parenthesis in the manner of an aside, introduced by a dash, in a poem that closes by unbuttoning itself grammatically, tenderly.

Chapter 6
Late travel poems

Bishop is the great travel poet of our modern era, and one reason why we keep returning to her poetry again and again. Travel, not just as subject matter, although it is certainly that from the time of her inaugural poem, 'The Map', in *North & South* (1946), to the designation of her last volume of poems as *Geography III* (1976), but as a line of verse possessing mobility of thought and realized in poetry that strives to be 'new, tender, quick'.

In this latter capacity, Bishop is quite unlike her many contemporaries who wrote frequently about their travels. Despite her love of small things and out-of-the-way places, hers are almost never postcard poems, snapshot scenes. (Her 'View of The Capitol from The Library of Congress' is a possible exception.) More often than not, Bishop's travel poems are motivated by reflecting—and reflecting on—the experience of travel, including the fate of the traveller, rather than on a scene or setting for its own sake. This gives a speculative edge to them, in keeping with their meditative, questioning quality signalled in the very choice of the title of her third volume, *Questions of Travel*. It is also in keeping with what we know about her process of composition involving three of her most famous late travel poems. Although their geneses differ, 'Crusoe in England', 'The Moose', and 'Santarém' were conceived over a number of years, with 'The Moose' dating as far back as a bus ride from Nova Scotia in August 1946. Among her longer poems—and 'Crusoe' is the longest of all her poems at 182 lines—they required more than just a sharp eye for description. They required a plot, an overarching idea generated by the separate challenges of the particular adventure that would give Bishop's lyric thinking full sail.

I want to conclude this *Very Short Introduction* by looking at these three late travel poems, in conjunction with a fourth, 'The End of March', which, along with 'Crusoe' and 'The Moose', was included in *Geography III*. ('Santarém' was first published in *The New Yorker* in 1978.) Given their richness, the chapter will be something of a Cook's tour. The poems are all remarkably different from one another, as we might expect. 'Crusoe in England' is a dramatic monologue based loosely on Defoe's eponymous traveller's daily life on a remote island. 'The Moose' describes an evening's winding bus journey through Nova Scotia into New Brunswick from the point of view of someone looking out the window. 'The End of March' is a 'walk poem' along the shore south of Boston, spoken by the poet. And 'Santarém' involves the memory of a journey up the Amazon, set at the 'conflux' of two great rivers in South America, the Amazon and the Tapajós. None of these poems is straightforward, with Bishop's penchant for zig-zags, for changing the rhythms of thought, achieving mythic realization in the 'dazzling dialectic' of 'Santarém'.

What all these journey poems have in common is an equation between lyric time and leisurely thinking, as suggested by Bishop in reference to a poem of Lowell's that appeared in *Near the Ocean* (1967). In a 1965 letter, she remarked, '"Walking Early Sunday Morning" has many wonderful things in it—and not the least, I think is the way it goes on in a leisurely way, like a Sunday morning—even if the meter is not leisurely, there seems to be *time*, to think—not like week-day thoughts.' The title of Lowell's poem is actually not 'Walking' but 'Waking Early Sunday Morning'. Whether this was a simple error in transcription or a creative misremembering, Bishop's late travel poems are conceived with a different notion of time from her waking poems. Above all, in their leisurely movement, they reflect '*time, to think*'. (Recall, by contrast, the urgently disruptive, waking 'cries galore' of 'Roosters'.) Bishop's travel poems fit their various metres to the extended occasion they are describing. They are, in a sense, always Sunday poems, and in their leisurely, lengthy explorations, they serve as a principal means whereby the famously reticent Bishop opens herself up as a subject in *Geography III*. As we've already seen, this is the more private Bishop of 'In the Waiting Room', 'One Art', and 'Poem', a careful unveiling in art that has made this final, slim volume not just a favourite among readers, but also something of a key to understanding her career retrospectively.

'One of it and one of me'

'Crusoe in England' is the saddest of all her poems, a poem of too many Sundays, too much time to think, and not enough Fridays (or Friday) for play. The full arc of the poem can only have come to Bishop fairly late in composition, after the death of Lota, since the poem is, at one level, an elegy in disguise, and in anticipation of her return to New England, a place associated in Bishop's mind with 'absolute loneliness', as once described to Lowell in 1948 in a series of letters about solitude and boredom. It included a memorable anecdote involving a remark made about her isolation by a local hairdresser: 'And when I'd said yes, I was an orphan, she said "Kind of awful, ain't it, ploughing through life alone". So now I can't walk downstairs in the morning or upstairs at night without feeling I'm ploughing. There's no place like New England.'

Here is the first of 'Crusoe's' 14 stanzas, which vary considerably in mood and length:

> A new volcano has erupted,
> the papers say, and last week I was reading
> where some ship saw an island being born:
> at first a breath of steam, ten miles away;

and then a black fleck—basalt, probably—
rose in the mate's binoculars
and caught on the horizon like a fly.
They named it. But my poor old island's still
un-rediscovered, un-renamable.
None of the books has ever got it right.

We might take this as an example of Bishop's late style—ruminative, meandering, frequently enjambed, as if thought is finding its way to the closing pentameter line, a single sentence where syntax and subject are grammatically sealed. Likewise, the poem's subject only gradually comes to the fore, a bit like the island itself, and when it does, it appears only as a negative construction. Scholars often talk about how Bishop's poem revises Defoe's providentially guided story in a sceptical direction, which it certainly does, but what catches our ear at this moment is the leisurely space opened up in that remarkable two-word pentameter line, 'un-rediscovered, un-renamable'. This is a speaker who likes to stretch out the line, who likes to hear the sound of his own voice—to discover by describing, rather than simply naming or renaming, the place he left behind many years prior.

Bishop's Crusoe is unusually garrulous, sometimes sounding even slightly inebriated: 'Well, I had fifty-two | miserable, small volcanoes I could climb | with a few slithery strides.' The gruff but slithery 'Well' opens up another opportunity for speech. We might liken our talker to Coleridge's 'ancient mariner who stoppeth one of three' or any number of wayward travellers from the past with a story to tell (perhaps Dante's Ulysses, emerging from the underworld, more than Tennyson's striving explorer). But Bishop's Crusoe remains *sui generis*. Sidling up to us, he shares something besides the constant hiss of turtles:

And I had waterspouts. Oh,
half a dozen at a time, far out,
they'd come and go, advancing and retreating,

their heads in cloud, their feet in moving patches
of scuffed-up white.
Glass chimneys, flexible, attenuated
sacerdotal beings of glass...I watched
the water spiral up in them like smoke.
Beautiful, yes, but not much company.

The description is certainly lyrical, 'beautiful' as the speaker says.
It develops from a 1943 letter to Marianne Moore ('I was sure
I had described waterspouts to you long ago'), written also from the
perspective of someone professing to be 'living in almost complete
solitude' (except she wasn't, of course, while writing to Moore).
But with a crucial difference, hinted at in the use of the concessive
'Oh'. Whereas epistolary Bishop describes the waterspouts
objectively, as Moore no doubt appreciated, here the poet
personifies nature throughout, even to the point of sanctification
('sacerdotal beings of glass' is added to the description) as a
compensatory sign for what her Crusoe so thoroughly lacks:
company. Do what he can to enliven it, Crusoe tells a story of
solitude and sameness, and, in his case, of the utter loneliness that
sameness begets: 'The sun set in the sea; the same odd sun | rose
from the sea, | And there was one of it and one of me.' A jingle
where the lightness—in several senses—underscores his isolation,
his uniqueness. Being *sui generis* isn't everything.

Not that Crusoe's story isn't moving or without comedy. Lowell
comments, 'Nothing you've written has such a mix of humor and
desperation.' But the narrator's account of solitude, including the
joke about failing to remember the line from Wordsworth's poem
"I wandered lonely as a cloud', is carefully plotted by the poet. The
phrase she can't remember speaks about 'the *bliss* of solitude' (my
italics). The jokes get darker by turns, become more violent in
response to the growing tedium. (See what happens to the red
berries in the course of the narrative, and to the baby goat.) The
longest portion of the narrative concludes, rather pointedly, with a
Darwinian bad dream of endless islands requiring Crusoe to live

on each, 'registering their flora, | their fauna, their geography'. This is surely the poet Bishop's nightmare, too—endless description, with no plot; just as the plan of dyeing the 'baby goat bright red...just to see | something a little different' backfires, ending on a note of anguish: 'And then his mother wouldn't recognize him'. As Lowell remarked, the poem is 'an analogue to your life, or an Ode to Dejection'. Looking ahead, we see it as both.

'Just when I thought I couldn't stand it | another minute longer, Friday came.' In Bishop's remaking of Defoe's story into her own, Friday, as she understands the person, is the missing subject, the 'un-rediscovered' discovered, the 'un-renamable' named: 'Friday was nice. | Friday was nice, and we were friends. | If only he had been a woman!' Critics have sometimes stood on their heads to do more with this deliberately flat description, but, in sharp contrast to the nightmare of endless description, it stands out in its Arcadian simplicity. The joke about Friday's gender comes as a relief as well. It works both ways, whether we think of the speaker as Defoe's heterosexual Crusoe or the voice of Bishop's lesbian desire speaking through him—and not a joke earlier Bishop would have made in print. For a moment, the poem has become something else. Not a vision of endless islands, it is lyrical in the original, pastoral sense of mixing innocence with desire, including, as in Virgil's second Eclogue, same-sex desire: 'He'd pet the baby goats sometimes, | and race with them, or carry one around. | —Pretty to watch; he had a pretty body.'

But only for a moment, and only as part of the governing narrative of loss, and not to be delayed by more fully developing Friday's character. 'And then one day they came and took us off.' There's more weight in that single, one-line paragraph than separate spacing can declare—Bishop at her most decisively reticent. It puts a full stop to the island fantasy. The poem shifts firmly back into the present tense, where it will remain in the final two paragraphs.

108

One consequence of that shift in tense is to point up the poem's initial temporal setting, which we might easily have forgotten by this time. But the return to the present also reminds us of the imaginative consequences of the two being removed from the island; that the whole poem has been conceived from the perspective of this slough of despond; that Crusoe's earlier ramblings are here to fill a vacancy, not because he is now in England but because he is in England—and has been for a long time—without Friday. The sense of loss, of grief, repressed for much of the poem, hasn't been forgotten. It is aired in the closing line, beginning with a dash that underscores the emotionally dislocated speaking subject '—And Friday, my dear Friday, died of measles | Seventeen years ago come March.'

Nothing more need be said, can be said, except to note how far the mind has travelled from the initial speck of a story found in a newspaper, and to recollect a precocious comment Bishop made in an undergraduate essay: 'The crises of our lives do not come, I think, accurately dated; they crop up unexpected and out of turn, and somehow or other arrange themselves according to a calendar we cannot control.' And so with the unexpected arrival and death of Friday, and the long monologue that comes into being as a result. 'I didn't realize how sad it is until I saw the proof—ye gods.' That is Bishop writing to Howard Moss about a poem that has come painfully back to life in the reading of it, as it does each time for us.

'This sweet | sensation of joy'

Some poems have to be completed before others can be ventured, and that may well be the case with 'Crusoe in England', the first published of these late travel poems. The evidence behind this assumption is simply Bishop's further exploration of travel as an engrossing, generally happier subject in poems of considerable length and accomplishment. Not that these poems don't have their points of resistance, but they see their way around or through them. The most charming is 'The Moose', as its status as one of her readers' favourite poems testifies. I mean 'charming' in the simple sense of fun to read (Bishop needn't have worried that 'simplicity is the biggest fault of this poem'). As a vehicle transporting people from one place to another, the imagined bus allows the reader to experience a variety of sounds and sights that temporarily come into precise focus one stanza at a time. There is the pleasure of naming, for instance, as we join the speaker in looking out the window:

> One stop at Bass River.
> Then the Economies—
> Lower, Middle, Upper;
> Five Islands, Five Houses,
> where a woman shakes a tablecloth
> out after supper.

The woman shaking the tablecloth is important for reminding us that we're reading more than a map—and the names of towns out of their actual order, as Bishop confessed to her editor. (She claimed to need a rhyme for 'supper'.) There is also comfort in the familiar:

> A woman climbs in
> with two market bags,
> brisk, freckled, elderly.
> 'A grand night. Yes, sir,
> all the way to Boston'.
> She regards us amicably.

Little requires commentary. What we see, or hear, is what we get—a high art of its own kind. The stanza is as perspicuous as glass, quietly cinematic in its framing, as the bus 'journeys west', amicably rhyming 'elderly' with 'amicably'.

But also 'charming' in the sense of magical, a topic Bishop had explored from a fluent, shamanistic perspective in 'The Riverman'.

In sharp contrast to the mundane account of the 1946 bus journey—'a dreadful trip', Bishop told Moore, in which, in the early morning, 'just as it was getting light, the driver had to stop suddenly for a big cow moose who was wandering down the road'—the poem repurposes this unexpected meeting to transport the reader from one level of reality to another. Via an archetypal journey through a seemingly 'impenetrable wood', the reader's usual expectations of the world—and likewise those of the travellers—are momentarily turned upside down and a new sense of reality emerges. (A familiar literary analogue, perhaps in the poem's background, is the effect the moonlit woods have in *A Midsummer Night's Dream*.) The effects are more complicated than producing accurate, spontaneous descriptions of the landscape, and Bishop shifts accordingly from primarily visual to auditory modes of representation, as overheard talk trails off into dream. Or rather, not dream, but sleep, from which a startled waking produces something more immediately real than a dream. The bus suddenly halts, the driver turns off the lights, as the poem throws a different, more intense spotlight on the poem's subject:

> A moose has come out of
> the impenetrable wood
> and stands there, looms, rather,
> in the middle of the road.
> It approaches; it sniffs at
> the bus's hot hood.
>
> Towering, antlerless,
> high as a church,
> homely as a house
> (or, safe as houses).
> A man's voice assures us
> 'Perfectly harmless....'
>
> Some of the passengers
> exclaim in whispers,

111

childishly, softly,
'Sure are big creatures.'
'It's awful plain.'
'Look! It's a she!'

Taking her time,
she looks the bus over,
grand, otherworldly.
Why, why do we feel
(we all feel) this sweet
sensation of joy?

Time seems to stop in the interest of heightening the encounter
with nature. The narrative of casual conversation, which
had been bordering on the apocalyptic—'things cleared up
finally'—breaks down under the pressure of the emerging
moment. Here, the speaker keeps adjusting her frame of
reference, from high to low, correcting herself, trying to be more
accurate; the bus driver delivers assurance that trails off into
space; the elderly people on the bus, offering multiple
perspectives, become children again in their whispers; and the
poet enters once more to speak for everybody, trying to
summarize the significance of this strange encounter with
something beyond the self. Whatever was simple earlier has
become suddenly complex, the synoptic view growing to
something of great constancy. 'Why, why do we feel | (we all
feel) this sweet | sensation of joy?' In comparison to Herbert
(or Hopkins), writes one appreciative reader, 'the moments of
joy in [Bishop's] poems are for smaller, more individual
epiphanies—and momentary ones'. True, but it is a long
moment of magical transformation on this occasion, 'grand,
otherworldly' in its lyric excess as Bishop dances around the
edges of revelation and ends this engagement, typically, with a
question that hovers over everything. Then both she and the bus
driver shift gears and go forward but not without one last look
back. Lyric has done its work in slowing the flow of time.

A kite string?—But no kite

Why, we might ask, does Bishop represent her fullest sense of community as being with other travellers also on the move? Perhaps the immediate occasion of 'The Moose' as first presented as the Phi Beta Kappa poem at Harvard's 1972 commencement influenced this road-of-life collective moment. But it's also not surprising that a poet who values thought in process is most at home in writing about travel, the subject again of 'The End of March' a few years later.

The poem belongs to a rich genre of 'walk' poems practised in the USA by the likes of Frost, Stevens, Williams, and many others. These are quest poems, and they often follow a general pattern in which the walker sets forth, arrives at a point, then frequently returns, with the goal being not the discovery of some holy grail, a woodpile, in Frost's case, or stumbling across a moose, in Bishop's, but to register the experience of change, and its significance, along the way on the speaker's consciousness. Think how different the trajectory of Bishop's poem would be if it bore the more definitive and portentous title 'The End of the March' rather than 'The End of March'. Her poem is about ordinary weather and change, inner and outer, a dilation on the old proverb that March comes in like a lion but goes out like what? a lamb? No, a refigured lion. Except it's not that simple because Bishop's thinking, like the life she led and the world she saw around her, is never single-tracked. Her lion, like her line, is a product of her readjustment.

That point is perhaps never made more clearly than in this poem, which does nothing if not feature loose ends, quite explicitly. Set between two stanzas describing the shoreline landscape are two interior stanzas. One is given over to detecting mysterious footprints in the sand (they look like those of a dog but seem the size of a lion), to observing lengths and lengths of endless 'wet white string', completely unlike the identically named 'wet white

113

string' in 'The Moose', to which the 'sweet peas cling'. This string unravels, 'looping up to the tide-line, down to the water, | over and over'. Although contrary to what we're told—thought, too, keeps looping back on itself in this poem—the string does end in a 'thick white snarl', but that only raises a further question or snarl: is it 'a kite string?—But no kite'. We still wonder as to its 'end'—its purpose. What can this tangle and entangling mean?

So, too, on a longer plane, the walker has apparently set out with an end in mind: 'I wanted to get as far as my proto-dream-house, | my crypto-dream-house'; 'crypto' complicates 'proto' by skewing it in the direction of a mystery. But after lavishly describing the house in the poem's longest section, Bishop tells us that she never arrived: 'that day the wind was much too cold | even to get that far, | and of course the house was boarded up'. What is then the purpose of the walk, and also the poem? Is Bishop being deliberately postmodern as she keeps undoing that which went before? Creating a journey ultimately without an end—in contrast, say, to Eliot's 'Journey of the Magi', which, though the magi had 'a cold coming of it', nonetheless did arrive and return?

In one sense, yes: Bishop never arrives at the point of return, nor, though retracing her steps, does she return to the point from where she set out. But that only puts greater pressure on the journey itself to do what walks can sometimes accomplish—indulge the imagination (as we've just seen with the footprints and strings), and not simply report what the eyes see: 'Here is a coast; here is a harbor' ('Arrival at Santos'). In Bishop's case, this means in part reorienting the original mood by turning the poem into a question of our understanding a shift in tone, always tricky with her, especially in the longest section involving the description of her dream house. The section, often read with strenuous attention to its prosody, includes a mixture of the realistic and the fantastic, the ludic and the practical, a game of filling out the desert island questionnaire as one would like it versus the one, say, Crusoe was

handed when he was shipwrecked. In this case, the fantasy
includes, à la Andrew Marvell's 'vegetable love' in 'The Garden',
'a sort of artichoke of a house, but greener | (boiled with
bicarbonate of soda?), | protected from spring tides by a palisade |
of—are they railroad ties?' The conceit here is quite different from
the epiphany generated by nature in 'The Moose'. However odd it
might strike others, oddness is part of the point. '(Many things
about this place are dubious)'. It is a list of your—or Bishop's—own
making, an account of the solitude enjoyed in retirement rather
than material for a Dejection Ode on the subject of loneliness.

It also means reorienting the role of the imagination to
incorporate a world of particulars, evident in the fantasy house
Bishop constructs—'There must be a stove; there *is* a chimney'—and
furthered in a yet more playfully deepening direction beginning
with the poem's prosy turn. 'On the way back our faces froze on
the other side.' Home is not on the horizon; it rarely is in Bishop;
but the comedy of leisure stemming from the imaginary house
continues on in the landscape:

> The sun came out for just a minute.
> For just a minute, set in their bezels of sand,
> the drab, damp, scattered stones
> were multi-colored,
> and all those high enough threw out long shadows,
> individual shadows, then pulled them in again.
> They could have been teasing the lion sun,
> except that now he was behind them
> —a sun who'd walked the beach the last low tide,
> making those big, majestic paw-prints,
> who perhaps had batted a kite out of the sky to play with.

Bishop's poems are often brilliantly packed and overflowing in
their close, and such is the case here. Frozen as her face is, the
landscape has brightened to the eye and mind. Indeed, prompted

in part by a Lowell comment, it is made brighter, firmer, and freer in the revisions that Bishop made to the original version that appeared in *The New Yorker*. Lines 2–4 in *The New Yorker* lack firm grounding and visual lustre ('and for a minute the embedded stones | showed what colours they were'), whereas the later version quoted above situates the moment more intensely through the repetition of the phrase 'for just a moment', giving the rest of the line, now transposed into 'bezels of sand', a place to go from in the further multi-coloration of 'the drab, damp, scattered stones'.

There is much at work here, including Bishop's recasting of Wallace Stevens's figure for the imagination as the 'lion of the spirit': 'the great cat [that] must stand potent in the sun' in 'An Ordinary Evening in New Haven'. In the last lines, 'an affectionate riposte', Bishop's lion sun comes forward playfully potent, as Bishop tacks back and forth from soundly-footed blank verse ('a **sun** who'd **walked** the **beach** the **last** low **tide**')—reminiscent of Milton's monosyllabic Son-sun line at the end of 'Lycidas' ('**Through** the dear **might** of **him** that **walked** the **waves**')—to the everyday prose of the lengthy, concluding line of the poem, one that, in its stretch, returns the 'kite' to view as 'perhaps' a figure for the now completed poem.

My 'perhaps' follows Bishop's. It is meant to leave open the possibility of reading the poem reflexively, as an allegory for the wayward process of the creative mind, always uncertain of its finish, always wary of lines 'rising on every wave, a sodden ghost, | falling back, sodden, giving up the ghost…. | A kite string?—But no kite'. This would be a poem, in other words, that never becomes 'new, tender, quick', to which the many unfinished versions in Bishop's archive offer ample testimony, but not the amply finished 'The *End* of March' (my italics). At the same time, the poem also leaves us with some simple advice, the kind Bishop liked to hand out to her friends, an emotional truth of a sort, of which she was often in need herself. Go for a walk, especially along a beach. It might change your mood, your inner weather, for the better.

Two rivers full of crazy shipping

'Santarém' may be Bishop's ultimate Sunday poem, not only because it mentions devotional subjects such as churches, nuns, priests, and the language of miracles, but because the poem is Bishop's purest, untrammelled representation of the mind in motion. 'Of course I may be remembering it all wrong | after, after—how many years?—' The poem's casually spoken first lines foreground the role of thinking by enacting its vagaries. Not errors of someone else's making (as in 'Crusoe in England'), these set the tone for accepting error, indeed for embracing error in the Latin root sense of wandering, and then seeing in the trope of wandering a metaphor for everything she likes about Santarém: 'I liked the place; I liked the idea of the place.'

Everything flows from this marriage of a person's mind with a place, as Bishop's verse tactfully meanders between the poem's two cognitive extremes: the Scylla of binary reductionism 'such as: life | death, right | wrong, male | female', and the Charybdis of self-assertion contained in Mr Swan's dismissive question at the poem's end: 'What's that ugly thing?' Bishop is constantly correcting herself, but always from slightly different angles ('Hadn't two rivers sprung | from the Garden of Eden? No, that was four | and they'd diverged'), even employing the rhetorical figure for correction in two different ways: the device of 'metanoi', meaning 'afterthought', for the first time she confuses church and cathedral, then again as 'epanorthosis' or 'emphatic correction', by enjambing the phrase across a stanza break and adding an exclamation point: 'the church | (Cathedral, rather!)'. 'The mind is stubborn, its will to wander difficult to control.' But the poet's skill in representing it is masterful, just when the casualness and corrections suggest the opposite.

What is surprising, even astonishing, about 'Santarém', and a source of ongoing wonder for this reader, is how well everything *is* remembered: the exact colour of the tiles, the '*shush, shush, shush*' sound of feet walking in sand, the 'widening zig-zag' on a tower 'struck by lightning', 'an empty wasps' nest', Mr Swan. Remembered, but also embellished by the selective memory as the travelling mind gains a golden distance on its original subject. Bishop's accepting speaker is everything the gnarled Crusoe is not, unconcerned with the daily mechanics of survival; concerned only with seeing in the place a reflection of the ideal, her ideal—in this case the absorption of the person, including the speaker, and a culture, a society, into the wider contours of an environment shaped by 'that conflux of two great rivers, Tapajós, Amazon, | grandly, silently flowing, flowing east'. Defined, that is, by change, historical change glimpsed in the remnant of the former slave-owners' 'blue eyes, English names, | and *oars*', people changing their minds, confusion, a cow 'being ferried | tipping, wobbling, somewhere, to be married', the absence of hierarchy river life fosters here, the comedy of people doing.

> A dozen or so young nuns, white-habited,
> waved gaily from an old stern-wheeler
> getting up steam, already hung with hammocks
> —off to their mission, days and days away
> up God knows what lost tributary.

Some readers have felt that 'Santarém' is 'suffused with allusions' to the Book of Revelation. If so, is it too much to suppose that, in Bishop's wandering imagination, at some apocalyptic point in the future all will become paddlers in the New Jerusalem 'up God knows what lost tributary'?

Even in Santarém, though, Sundays come to an end. 'Then—my ship's whistle blew. I couldn't stay.' Bishop's exit startles slightly—there had been no mention of her means of travel earlier—but not before she discovers a souvenir, 'an empty wasps' nest'. 'Small, exquisite, clean matte white, | and hard as stucco', she takes it with her as part of a simple but complicated gift

118

exchange with the local pharmacist, in which contemplation wins out over commerce. She admires it, he gives it to her. An aura of wonder lingers. She's not a tourist but a traveller, an observer in the mode of Marianne Moore, and yet more than that too, as we know, since the stucco-like hardness of the nest also throws a contrasting light on the poem we have been reading with regard to movement and change. It is left to the utilitarian 'Mr. Swan, | Dutch, the retiring head of Philips Electric', something of an 'old stern-wheeler', to supply the efficient swan song: 'What's that ugly thing?' Even the contraction argues haste. We've entered a different time zone.

I spoke earlier of 'Crusoe in England' as an example of Bishop's late style. The style of 'Santarém' seems later still, more verbally opulent and burnished, instinctively allied with its fluvial surroundings, which supplies a vocabulary for describing Bishop's art. But it's a late poem, not a last poem, not even Bishop's last poem about Brazil. She would shortly publish her pastoral elegy to Lowell, 'North Haven', also about mutability, and soon after that her scathing 'Pink Dog', although she would not live to see her little 'Sonnet' into print. But 'Santarém' is her last travel poem. It is a bit like her moose, 'grand and otherworldly', with the trope of travel serving as a figure for the questing, questioning mind that we think of as Elizabeth Bishop.

Epilogue

It is customary for an academic book to acknowledge somewhere the professional organizations and affiliations that underlie the final version, but in this particular book many of the ideas come from the classroom. For a number of years, I taught Bishop in a seminar called, simply, 'How to Read a Poem'. Readings ranged from Sir Thomas Wyatt to the present day and were amplified by the regular series of poetry readings offered at the UCLA-Hammer Museum in Los Angeles. In conjunction with the medley of disparate poems sampled across the centuries each week, we also read continuously from the works of two poets. Year after year, Elizabeth Bishop was always one of the two poets.

As all lists do, this one reflected the instructor's preferences, and although readings changed over time, the goal of the class remained largely the same: to have students discover how to speak and write about what the eye sees and the ear hears when a poem on a page is put before them. A simple request. Although it had a New Critical aspect to it—the poem was the central focus of discussion—it ruled in many of the thoughts that New Criticism, in its stricter form, ruled out. But the task was also not an easy one. In part, this is because the phenomenon of the visual today has overtaken and absorbed the attention of so many, whether young or old. (Congruent with this seminar was a graduate class taught by a distinguished musicologist who felt a similar need to teach notation.) But it is also owing to how knowledge is often thematically or historically organized in universities, where texts in the humanities assume a place in a hierarchy of approaches often established by the social sciences. And, of course, it is because talking about those black marks on the page is, and always has been, an unnatural task, an acquired art. It requires considerable learning and practice. The aim of the course was to have students resist seeing *through* the poem in their desire to replicate a version of their own assumed reality, however arrived at, and to do so by attending to the grammatical signs on the page that educated them in how to read the work at hand. One kind of resistance met with another, which is where the excitement is, and learning begins.

And here, too, is where Bishop comes in. She was the star of the seminar—always, and not simply because students liked to read about fish in the poem of that title. Many didn't know anything about fishing and still don't, but a number now do know how to read a poem about a fish because Bishop is so good at taking you through the steps. First step, look closely; second step, look closer still; third step look even more closely, but especially now with an eye to where the poem is going, not to where you think it should be going, but where its diction, syntax, grammar, and punctuation lead. This means listening to the poem, bringing the ear out of hiding in order to help the eye to see and the mind to think. Bishop's poems are always about surfaces getting deeper, about knowledge as process. She lets the fish go at the end of the poem. Does it matter? Not as much as the getting there. There is a technical language for expressing this experience, this journey, some of which I use in this book; but not all discourses find their way equally into this study (they never do), which is one of the benefits of having a section marked 'Further reading'.

Does Bishop age well? Better than most, but we're all bound by our histories and by History; the past can flow into but never be the present. Why read Bishop? Because she brings out the inner poet in all of us. Why do we feel this way? Because we do. That's what reading a poem about a moose does. It makes us feel that we're all there as part of the poem's creative energy at the moment of its arriving.

Timeline

1846	William Brown Bulmer, EB's maternal grandfather, born
1871	Elizabeth Hutchinson, EB's maternal grandmother (b. 1850), marries William Brown Bulmer in Great Village, Nova Scotia
1879	Gertrude Bulmer, EB's mother, born in Great Village, Nova Scotia, the Bulmers' 4th child. Surviving siblings include: Maude (b. 1873), Arthur (b. 1876), Grace (b. 1889), and Mary (b. 1900)
1885	Ezra Pound born
1887	Marianne Moore born
1888	T. S. Eliot born
1908	Gertrude Bulmer marries William Thomas Bishop (b. 1872) of Worcester, Massachusetts; son of John W. Bishop and Sarah Foster
1911	Elizabeth Bishop born on 8 February; father dies of Bright's disease on 13 October
1916	Gertrude Bulmer suffers mental breakdown and is hospitalized at the Nova Scotia Hospital in Dartmouth, NS. EB remains with maternal grandmother in Great Village
1917	EB taken to Worcester, Massachusetts, to live with paternal grandparents; Robert Lowell born

1918	EB moves in with her aunt, Maude Bulmer Shepherdson, and uncle, George Shepherdson, in Revere, Massachusetts. First World War ends
1922	Publication of T. S. Eliot's *The Waste Land*
1923	Publication of Wallace Stevens's *Harmonium*
1924	Publication of Marianne Moore's *Observations*
1924–9	Attends Chequesett Summer Camp, Cape Cod
1926	Attends North Shore Country Day School in Swampscott, Massachusetts
1927–30	Attends Walnut Hill School in Natick, Massachusetts
1930–4	Attends Vassar College; in the company of future writers Eleanor Clark and Mary McCarthy, founds the short-lived literary magazine *Con Spirito*; publishes in *The Vassar Review*; interviews T. S. Eliot during his campus visit for the *Vassar Miscellany*
1934	Through the auspices of the Vassar Librarian, Fanny Borden, meets Marianne Moore outside the New York Public Library on 16 March. Mother dies on 29 May
1935	Reads extensively in the New York Public Library; first trip to Europe and North Africa with Louise Crane
1936	First trip to Florida with Louise Crane
1937	Returns to Europe with Crane; car accident in France involving Margaret Miller; Picasso paints *Guernica*
1938	Returns to Florida and buys house in Key West, Florida, on 624 White Street, now a registered Literary Landmark owned by the Key West Literary Seminar
1939	Outbreak of Second World War
1941	Begins six-year relationship with Marjorie Stevens
1942	Travels to Mexico with Stevens, meets Pablo Neruda
1945	Second World War ends
1946	Returns to Nova Scotia in July; in August, Bishop's first book of poems, *North & South*, is published, having won the Houghton Mifflin Poetry Prize the previous year; meets Lowell, who receives Pulitzer Prize for *Lord Weary's Castle*

1947	Awarded Guggenheim Fellowship; travels to Cape Breton, Nova Scotia; begins treatment for alcoholism, asthma, and depression with Dr Anny Baumann; at Baumann's suggestion, corresponds with the psychiatrist Ruth Foster
1949	Begins year-long appointment as Consultant in Poetry at the Library of Congress; visits Pound in St Elizabeths
1950	Resident fellow at Yaddo writers colony; meets May Swenson and Beauford Delaney
1951	In November, travels to South America on the Norwegian freighter SS *Bowplate*. Visits Lota de Macedo Soares in Rio de Janeiro, Brazil, and spends the next 16 years in Brazil with Lota
1955	Publication of *Poems*, which includes *A Cold Spring* and a reissue of *North & South*
1956	Receives Pulitzer Prize for *Poems: North & South—A Cold Spring*
1957	Publication of her translation of *The Diary of Helena Morley*
1958	Travels to Brasilia, in the company of Aldous and Laura Huxley, which includes an excursion to see the Uialapita tribe living on a tributary of the Xingo River
1959	Lowell publishes *Life Studies*, which receives The National Book Award
1960	Travels a thousand miles down the Amazon River on the *Lauro Sodré*, from Manaus to Belém, visiting Santarém along the way
1961	Macedo Soares begins what proves to be a long, difficult period overseeing the construction of the large city park, Parque do Flamengo, on the Rio waterfront
1962	Publication of *Brazil*, written by Bishop but considerably changed by the editors for *Life*'s World Library Series
1964	Elected to the Academy of American Poets; translates and publishes three stories by Clarise Lispector in the *Kenyon Review*
1965	Publication of *Questions of Travel*; purchases colonial house in need of restoration in the small baroque city of Ouro Prêto

1966	Teaches for a semester at the University of Washington, Seattle; begins a relationship with Roxanne Cumming; Machedo Soares hospitalized
1967	On 3 July, Bishop flies to New York; against her doctor's advice, Macedo Soares follows in September but overdoses on valium and, after going into a coma, dies on 25 September
1968	Lives in San Francisco with Roxanne Cumming and her son. Meets Thom Gunn and Robert Duncan
1969	Publication of *The Complete Poems*
1970	Receives National Book Award for *The Complete Poems*; begins teaching at Harvard; meets Alice Methfessel
1971	Returns for several months to Ouro Prêto; travels with Alice to the Galápagos Islands and Machu Picchu
1972	Marianne Moore dies. Publication of *An Anthology of Twentieth-Century Brazilian Poetry*, edited with Emanuel Brasil
1974	Purchases a condominium at Lewis Wharf on the Boston Waterfront; begins spending summers at Sabine Farm on the island of North Haven off the Maine Coast
1976	Awarded Newstadt International Prize for Literature. *Geography III* published; receives National Book Critics Circle Award
1977	Robert Lowell dies, 12 September, his passing commemorated in Bishop's pastoral elegy, 'North Haven'
1978	Awarded second Guggenheim Fellowship
1979	Receives honorary degree from Dalhousie University, Nova Scotia. 6 October, dies suddenly of a cerebral aneurysm at Lewis Wharf
1991	Elizabeth Bishop Society (USA) is formed
1994	Elizabeth Bishop Society of Nova Scotia, Canada, is formed

References

All quotations from Bishop's poems are from *Elizabeth Bishop: Poems* (Farrar, Straus, and Giroux, 2011).

Note on Abbreviations

LOA   Elizabeth Bishop*: Poems, Prose, and Letters*, ed. Robert Giroux and Lloyd Schwartz (The Library of America, 2008).

NYer *Elizabeth Bishop and The New Yorker: The Complete Correspondence*, ed. Joelle Biele (Farrar, Straus, and Giroux, 2011).

OA   Elizabeth Bishop, *One Art: Letters*, ed. Robert Giroux (Farrar, Straus, and Giroux, 1994).

WIA   *Words in Air: The Complete Correspondence between Elizabeth Bishop and Robert Lowell*, ed. Thomas Travisano with Saskia Hamilton (Farrar, Straus, and Giroux, 2008).

Chapter 1: Less is more: a world in miniature

'most beloved', from John Felstiner, *Can Poetry Save the Earth? A Field Guide to Nature Poems* (Yale University Press, 2009), 228.

'I like the way her whole oeuvre', from 'James Merrill, An Interview', in Lloyd Schwartz and Sybil P. Estess (eds), *Elizabeth Bishop and her Art* (University of Michigan, 1983), 200.

'Lowell was a white Anglo-Saxon', from Dennis O'Driscoll, *Stepping Stones: Interviews with Seamus Heaney* (Farrar, Straus, and Giroux, 2008), 280.

'discovering a new planet', from Tom Paulin, 'Writing to the Moment', in *Writing to the Moment: Collected Critical Essays, 1980–1996* (Faber and Faber, 1998), 215.

'The gravestone would also come to bear the words', see the 'Coda: All The Untidy Activity Continues', in Thomas Travisano, *Love Unknown: The Life and Worlds of Elizabeth Bishop* (Viking, 2019).

'"total recall" of Nova Scotia', from *OA*, 249: EB to Kit and Ilse Barker 12 October 1952.

'the three qualities I admire in the poetry I like best', from *LOA*, 703.

'After the first death', from Dylan Thomas, 'A Refusal to Mourn the Death, by Fire, of a Child in London'.

'with regard to her mother in "The Country Mouse"'; see *LOA*, 425.

'The sudden release of the last line', from Howard Moss, 'All Praise', *The Kenyon Review* 28.2 (March 1966), 261.

Chapter 2: Formal matters

'*rumba* rhythm', from *WIA*, 346: EB to Robert Lowell (RL) (October 1960).

'As one reader notes'; the perception belongs to Eleanor Cook, *Elizabeth Bishop at Work* (Harvard University Press, 2016), 96.

'*literatura de cordel…*', from Barbara Page, 'Home, Wherever That May Be: Poems and Prose of Brazil', in Angus Cleghorn and Jonathan Ellis (eds), *The Cambridge Companion to Elizabeth Bishop* (Cambridge University Press, 2014), 137.

'"The Burglar of Babylon" Bishop's "best" poem', from *WIA*, 563: EB to RL, 11 December 1964; and *OA*, 431: EB to Randall Jarrell, 25 February 1965.

'it "gives more of Brazil somehow"', from *WIA*, 560: RL to EB, 22 November 1964.

'The eye of the outsider', from Adrienne Rich, 'The Eye of the Outsider', *Boston Review* (April 1983), 15–17.

'daringly messy', from Thom Gunn, 'In and out of the box', *TLS* July 27–2 August 1990, 791.

'a bad case of the *Threes*', from *OA*, 96: EB to Marianne Moore, 17 October 1940.

'blank verse *moo*', from *OA*, 48: EB to Marianne Moore, 5 December 1936.

'And one thing more', from *OA*, 12: EB to Donald Stanford, 20 November 1933.

'self-conscious modernism', from J. Max Patrick and Robert O. Evans, with John M. Wallace (eds), *Essays by Morris J. Croll, 'Attic' and Baroque Prose Style* (Princeton University Press, 1966), 203.

'the first poet successfully to use all the resources of prose', from Vidyan Ravinthiran, *Elizabeth Bishop's Prosaic* (Bucknell University Press, 2015), 1.

'a type of stylized collage', from *Elizabeth Bishop's Prosaic*, 11.

Chapter 3: 'The Armadillo', the art of description, and 'Brazil, January 1, 1502'

'billfold and occasionally amaze people with it'; this and the next four quotations, from *WIA*, 324: RL to EB, 28 April 1960; 591: RL to EB, 28 October 1965; 517: RL to EB, 24 January 1964; 230: RL to EB, 11 September 1957; and 466: EB to RL, 17 June 1963.

'endless "description"', from *NYer*, 386: EB to Howard Moss, 1 October 1977.

'Many of your poems start obliquely', from *WIA*, 760: RL to EB, 22 February 1974.

'I see the bomb', from *WIA*, 591: RL to EB, 28 October 1965.

'I am glad you like "*The Armadillo*"', from *NYer*, 181: EB to Howard Moss, 3 September 1956.

'As far as I know'; this and other quotations, from 'As We Like It: Miss Moore and the Delight of Imitation', *LOA*, 680–6.

'It's like the Four Horsemen', from *The New Yorker*, 11 November 2019, 42.

'with Lowell again leading the way', in *WIA*, 307: RL to EB, 4 January 1960.

'How I envy the historical stretch at the end', from *WIA*, 591: RL to EB, 28 October 1965.

'I am so glad you liked the New Year's poem', from *WIA*, 310, EB to RL, 15 February 1960.

Chapter 4: Poetry and painting

'her *Poems* seems to me', from *Harper's Magazine*, 1 October 1955, 98.

'[Your review] has made me so happy', from *OA*, 312: EB to Randall Jarrell, 26 December 1955.

'lived experience', from Siobhan Phillips, 'Bishop's Correspondence', in Angus Cleghorn and Jonathan Ellis (eds), *The Cambridge*

Companion to Elizabeth Bishop (Cambridge University Press, 2014), 158.

'Bishop was Dutch in her love of curiosities', from the 'Afterword' to David Kalstone, *Becoming A Poet: Elizabeth Bishop with Marianne Moore and Robert Lowell* (Farrar, Straus, and Giroux, 1989), 258.

'the violent roosters Picasso did', from *OA*, 96: EB to Marianne Moore, 17 October 1940.

'that strange kind of modesty', from *WIA*, 250: EB to RL, 29 January 1958.

'Thousands of abstractions', from *OA*, 376–7: EB to Pearl Kazin, 24 October 1959.

'on sheets of paper', from William Benton (ed.), *Exchanging Hats: Elizabeth Bishop Paintings* (Farrar, Straus, and Giroux, 1996), xviii.

'a peculiar and captivating freshness, flatness, and remoteness', from 'Gregorio Valdes, 1879–1939', in *LOA*, 332.

'possibly her masterpiece', from Lloyd Schwartz and Sybil P. Estess (eds), *Elizabeth Bishop and her Art* (University of Michigan Press, 1983), 203.

'characterized by a fascination with the bizarre', from Ian Chilvers and Harold Osborn (eds), *The Oxford Dictionary of Art* (2nd edn, Oxford University Press, 1997), 544.

'I have disliked', from *OA*, 135: EB to Ferris Greenslet, 19 April 1946.

'Dreams, works of art…', from *LOA*, 861: EB to Anne Stevenson, 8 January 1964.

'an acknowledged debt to Max Ernst's *Histoire naturelle*', in *OA*, 478: EB to Joseph Summers, 19 October 1967.

'It is a great relief…', from *LOA*, 469 ('Wesley Wehr').

'notional', from John Hollander, *The Gazer's Spirit: Poems Speaking to Silent Works of Art* (University of Chicago Press, 1995).

'one of the five poems I wish I had written', from BBC Radio 3, Tuesday, 26 September 2017.

'in caps or lower case'; this and the following remarks are from *NYer*, 13–15.

'Here's an old-fashioned…' and Moss's responses, from *NYer*, 339: EB to Howard Moss, 28 March 1972.

Chapter 5: Love known

'at least I don't *feel* as if I wrote that way', from *OA*, 262, EB to Pearl Kazin, 25 April 1953.

'I want closets', from Gary Fountain and Peter Brazeau (eds),
    Remembering Elizabeth Bishop: An Oral Biography (University of
    Massachusetts Press, 1994), 330.

'A little fey, even precious', from Margaret Dickie, *Stein, Bishop &
    Rich: Lyrics of Love, War, & Place* (University of North Carolina
    Press, 1997), 92.

'sexual courage', from *LOA*, 729.

'passionately personal', from Alan Williamson, '*A Cold Spring*: The Poet
    of Feeling', in Lloyd Schwartz and Sybil P. Estess (eds), *Elizabeth
    Bishop and her Art* (University of Michigan Press, 1983), 96.

'The "Four Poems" are certainly fragmentary', from *OA*, 308, EB to
    U.T. and Joseph Summers, 18 July 1955.

'"strong-stress" metre of Anglo-Saxon poetry'; see Eleanor
    Cook, *Elizabeth Bishop at Work* (Harvard University Press,
    2016), 133.

'a sketch for an acute, neurotic, "modern" drama', from *LOA*, 805, EB
    to May Swenson, 6 September 1955.

'couldn't understand', from *OA*, 241, EB to Pearl Kazin, 8 July 1952.

'This is an after-the-fact poem by a coy mistress', from Peter Robinson,
    'Pretended Acts: "The Shampoo"', in Linda Anderson and Jo
    Shapcott (eds), *Elizabeth Bishop: Poet of the Periphery* (Newcastle/
    Bloodaxe, 2002), 105.

'I guess the deciding factor', from *NYer*, xxv.

Lowell's and Bishop's remarks about 'Song for the Rainy Season', from
    WIA, 343 and 346, respectively.

'I am having a poem in your magazine fairly soon', from *NYer*, 378, EB
    to Katharine White, 16 January 1976.

'It was like writing a letter', this and the 16 drafts of 'One Art' can be
    found in Alice Quinn (ed.), *Edgar Allan Poe & The Juke Box:
    Uncollected Poems, Drafts, and Fragments* (Farrar, Straus, and
    Giroux, 2006), 223 *passim*.

'Everyone is moved to tears by it', from *LOA*, 704.

Chapter 6: Late travel poems

'new, tender, quick', from George Herbert's 'Love Unknown', quoted by
    James Merrill in 'Overdue Pilgrimage to Nova Scotia', in
    J. D. McClatchy and Stephen Yenser (eds), *James Merrill: Collected
    Poems* (Alfred A. Knopf, 2002), 666.

'"Walking Early Sunday Morning" has many wonderful things in it',
    from *WIA*, 587–8, EB to RL, 19 September 1965.

'absolute loneliness', from *WIA*, 38–9, EB to RL, 30 June 1948; 'And when I'd said yes', from *WIA*, 42, 11 July 1948.

'Nothing you've written', from *WIA*, 755, letter, RL to EB, 31 July 1973.

'the crisis of our lives', from 'Dimensions for a Novel', *LOA*, 677.

'I didn't realize how sad it is', from *NYer*, 331–2, EB to Howard Moss, 24 June 1971.

'simplicity is the biggest fault of this poem', *NYer*, 346, EB to Howard Moss, 7 July 1972.

'a dreadful trip', from *OA*, 141: EB to Marianne Moore, 29 August 1946.

'the moments of joy in [Bishop's] poems', from Joseph Summers, 'George Herbert and Elizabeth Bishop', in Jonathan F. S. Post and Sidney Gottlieb (eds), *George Herbert in the Nineties: Reflections and Reassessments* (George Herbert Journal, Studies & Monographs, 1995), 55.

'"walk" poems'; see Roger Gilbert, *Walks in the World: Representation and Experience in Modern American Poetry* (Princeton, 1991), 29.

'prompted in part by a Lowell comment', from *WIA*, 768–9, RL to EB, 6 October 1974; Bishop's versions of the last stanza are in *NYer*, l–li.

'suffused with allusions', from Eleanor Cook, *Elizabeth Bishop at Work* (Harvard University Press, 2016), 257.

Further reading

General criticism and commentary

Biographies

Remembering Elizabeth Bishop: An Oral Biography, ed. Gary Fountain and Peter Brazeau (University of Massachusetts Press, 1994).

Megan Marshall, *Elizabeth Bishop: A Miracle for Breakfast* (Houghton Mifflin Harcourt, 2017).

Brett C. Millier, *Elizabeth Bishop: Life and the Memory of It* (University of California Press, 1993).

Thomas Travisano, *Love Unknown: The Life and Worlds of Elizabeth Bishop* (Viking, 2019).

Anthologies

Anthology of Twentieth-Century Brazilian Poetry, ed. Elizabeth Bishop and Emanuel Brasil (Wesleyan University Press, 1972).

Exchanging Hats: Elizabeth Bishop: Paintings, ed. William Benton (Farrar, Straus, and Giroux, 1996).

Monographs

Linda Anderson, *Elizabeth Bishop: Lines of Connection* (Edinburgh University Press, 2013).

Eleanor Cook, *Elizabeth Bishop at Work* (Harvard University Press, 2016).

Laurel Snow Corelle, *A Poet's High Argument: Elizabeth Bishop and Christianity* (University of South Carolina Press, 2008).

Bonnie Costello, *Elizabeth Bishop: Questions of Mastery* (Harvard University Press, 1991).

C. K. Doreski, *Elizabeth Bishop: The Restraints of Language* (Oxford University Press, 1993).

Jonathan Ellis, *Art and Memory in the Work of Elizabeth Bishop* (Ashgate, 2006).

Lorrie Goldensohn, *Elizabeth Bishop: The Biography of Poetry* (Columbia University Press, 1992).

Victoria Harrison, *Elizabeth Bishop's Poetics of Intimacy* (Cambridge University Press, 1993).

Bethany Hicok, *Elizabeth Bishop's Brazil* (University of Virginia Press, 2016).

David Kalstone, *Becoming a Poet: Elizabeth Bishop with Marianne Moore and Robert Lowell* (Farrar, Straus, Giroux, 1989).

Susan McCabe, *Elizabeth Bishop: Her Poetics of Loss* (Pennsylvania State University Press, 1994).

Mariana Machova, *Elizabeth Bishop and Translation* (Lexington Books, 2017).

Jeredith Merrin, *An Enabling Humility: Marianne Moore, Elizabeth Bishop, and the Uses of Tradition* (Rutgers University Press, 1990).

Zachariah Pickard, *Elizabeth Bishop's Poetics of Description* (McGill-Queen's University Press, 2009).

Vidyan Ravinthiran, *Elizabeth Bishop's Prosaic* (Bucknell University Press, 2015).

Camille Roman, *Elizabeth Bishop's World War II–Cold War View* (Palgrave, 2001).

Peggy Samuels, *Deep Skin: Elizabeth Bishop and Visual Art* (Cornell University Press, 2010).

Anne Stevenson, *Elizabeth Bishop* (Twayne Publishers, 1966).

Anne Stevenson, *Five Looks at Elizabeth Bishop* (Bellew Publishing Co., Ltd, 1998).

Thomas J. Travisano, *Elizabeth Bishop: Her Artistic Development* (University of Virginia Press, 1988).

Colm Tóibín, *On Elizabeth Bishop* (Princeton University Press, 2015).

Cheryl Walker, *God and Elizabeth Bishop: Meditations on Religion and Poetry* (Palgrave, 2005).

Essay collections

Linda Anderson and Jo Shapcott (eds), *Elizabeth Bishop: Poet of the Periphery* (Bloodaxe Books Ltd, 2002).

Angus Cleghorn and Jonathan Ellis (eds), *The Cambridge Companion to Elizabeth Bishop* (Cambridge University Press, 2014).

Angus Cleghorn, Bethany Hicok, and Thomas Travisano (eds), *Elizabeth Bishop in the Twenty-First Century: Reading the New Editions* (University of Virginia Press, 2012).

Gwendolyn Davies, Sandra Barry, and Peter Sanger (eds), *Divisions of the Heart: Elizabeth Bishop and the Art of Memory and Place* (Gaspereau Press, 2001).

Jonathan Ellis (ed.), *Reading Elizabeth Bishop: An Edinburgh Companion* (Edinburgh University Press, 2019).

Bethany Hicok (ed.), *Elizabeth Bishop and the Literary Archive* (Lever Press, 2019).

Marilyn May Lombardi (ed.), *Elizabeth Bishop: The Geography of Gender* (University Press of Virginia, 1993).

Lloyd Schwartz and Sybil P. Estess (eds), *Elizabeth Bishop and her Art* (University of Michigan Press, 1983).

Chapter 1: Less is more: a world in miniature

Linda Anderson, 'Disturbances of the Archive: Repetition and Memory in Elizabeth Bishop's Poetry', in Jonathan Ellis (ed.), *Reading Elizabeth Bishop: An Edinburgh Companion* (Edinburgh University Press, 2019), 19–32.

Sandra Barry, 'In the Village: Bishop and Nova Scotia', in Angus Cleghorn and Jonathan Ellis (eds), *The Cambridge Companion to Elizabeth Bishop* (Cambridge University Press, 2014), 97–110.

Elizabeth Bishop, 'In the Village', *LOA*, 99–118.

Elizabeth Bishop, 'The Country Mouse', *LOA*, 410–26.

Elizabeth Bishop, 'Gwendolyn', *LOA*, 605–16.

Elizabeth Bishop, 'Memories of Uncle Neddy', *LOA*, 617–36.

Elizabeth Bishop, 'Primer Class', *LOA*, 402–9.

Marvin Campbell, 'Elizabeth Bishop and Audre Lorde: Two Views of "Florida", in the Global South Atlantic', in Jonathan Ellis (ed.), *Reading Elizabeth Bishop: An Edinburgh Companion* (Edinburgh University Press, 2019), 280–93.

Marvin Campbell, 'Elizabeth Bishop and Race in the Archive', in Bethany Hicok (ed.), *Elizabeth Bishop and the Literary Archive* (Lever Press, 2019), 131–50.

Betsy Erkkila, 'Elizabeth Bishop, Modernism, and the Left', *American Literary History* 8.2 (Summer 1996), 284–310.

Langdon Hammer, 'Useless Concentration: Life and Work in Elizabeth Bishop's Letters and Poems', *American Literary History* 9.1 (Spring 1997), 162–80.

William Logan, 'Elizabeth Bishop at Summer Camp', *Virginia Quarterly Review* 88 (Spring 2012), 52–87.

George Monteiro (ed.), *Conversations with Elizabeth Bishop* (University Press of Mississippi, 1996).

Heather Treseler, 'Dreaming in Color: Bishop's Notebook Letter-Poems', in Angus Cleghorn, Bethany Hicok, and Thomas Travisano (eds), *Elizabeth Bishop in the Twenty-First Century: Reading the New Editions* (University of Virginia Press, 2012), 88–103.

Chapter 2: Formal matters

Elizabeth Bishop, 'Time's Andromeda', *LOA*, 641–59.

Elizabeth Bishop, 'Gerard Manley Hopkins, Notes on Timing in his Poetry', *LOA*, 660–7.

Elizabeth Bishop, 'Writing poetry is an unnatural act...' *LOA*, 702–6.

Elizabeth Bishop, 'Efforts of Affection: A Memoir of Marianne Moore', *LOA*, 471–99.

Elizabeth Bishop, 'A Sentimental Tribute: Marianne Moore', *LOA*, 707–11.

Elizabeth Bishop, 'A Brief Reminiscence and a Brief Tribute', *LOA*, 728–31. (On Marianne Moore and W. H. Auden.)

Bonnie Costello, 'Bishop and the Poetic Tradition', in Angus Cleghorn and Jonathan Ellis (eds), *The Cambridge Companion to Elizabeth Bishop* (Cambridge University Press, 2014), 79–94.

Jess Cotton, '"Solid cuteness": Elizabeth Bishop's Art of Simplicity', in Jonathan Ellis (ed.), *Reading Elizabeth Bishop: An Edinburgh Companion* (Edinburgh University Press, 2019), 149–63.

Penelope Laurans, '"Old Correspondences": Prosodic Transformations in Elizabeth Bishop', in Lloyd Schwartz and Sybil P. Estess (eds), *Elizabeth Bishop and her Art* (University of Michigan Press, 1983), 75–95.

James Longenbach, *Modern Poetry after Modernism* (Oxford University Press, 1997), 22–34 ('Elizabeth Bishop's Bramble Bushes').

Tom Paulin, 'Crusoe Revisited: Elizabeth Bishop', in *Crusoe's Secret: The Aesthetic of Dissent* (Faber & Faber, 2005), 332–48.

Jonathan F. S. Post, 'The Baroque and Elizabeth Bishop', *The John Donne Journal* 21 (2002), 101–33.

Chapter 3: 'The Armadillo', the art of description, and 'Brazil, January 1, 1502'

Elizabeth Bishop, *Brazil* (Time Life Books, 1962).

Jacqueline Vaught Brogan, 'Mapping Elizabeth Bishop's "Brazil, January 1, 1502"', *Texas Studies in Language and Literature* 59 (Spring 2017), 106–35.

Kim Fortuna, 'Elizabeth Bishop's "Pink Dog" and Other Non-human Animals', *Textual Practice* (Routledge) 29.6 (2015), 1099–116.

Bethany Hicok, *Elizabeth Bishop's Brazil* (University of Virginia Press, 2016).

Zachariah Pickard, *Elizabeth Bishop's Poetics of Description* (McGill-Queen's University Press, 2009).

Chapter 4: Poetry and painting

Lorrie Goldensohn, 'The Homeless Eye', in Gwendolyn Davies, Sandra Barry, and Peter Sanger (eds), *Divisions of the Heart: Elizabeth Bishop and the Art of Memory and Place* (Gaspereau Press, 2001), 103–11.

Jane Hedley, Nick Halpern, and Willard Spiegelman (eds), *In the Frame: Women's Ekphrastic Poetry from Marianne Moore to Susan Wheeler* (University of Delaware Press, 2009).

J. D. McClatchy, *Poets on Painters: Essays on the Art of Painting by Twentieth-Century Poets* (University of California Press, 1988).

Susan Rosenbaum, 'The Case of the Falling *S*: Elizabeth Bishop, Visual Poetry and the International Avant-Garde', in Jonathan Ellis (ed.), *Reading Elizabeth Bishop: An Edinburgh Companion* (Edinburgh University Press, 2019), 177–93.

Peggy Samuels, 'Bishop and Visual Art', in Angus Cleghorn and Jonathan Ellis (eds), *The Cambridge Companion to Elizabeth Bishop* (Cambridge University Press, 2014), 169–82.

Willard Spiegelman, *How Poets See the World: The Art of Description in Contemporary Poetry* (Oxford University Press, 2005).

Chapter 5: Love known

Lorrie Goldensohn, 'Bishop's Posthumous Publications', in Angus Cleghorn and Jonathan Ellis (eds), *The Cambridge Companion to Elizabeth Bishop* (Cambridge University Press, 2014), 183–96.

Kathryn R. Kent, *Making Girls into Women: American Women's Writing and the Rise of Lesbian Identity* (Duke University Press, 2003).

Marilyn May Lombardi, 'The Closet of Breath: Elizabeth Bishop, her Body and her Art', in Marilyn Mary Lombardi (ed.), *Elizabeth Bishop: The Geography of Gender* (University Press of Virginia, 1993), 46–69.

Susan McCabe, 'Survival of the Queerly Fit: Darwin, Marianne Moore, and Elizabeth Bishop', *Twentieth-Century Literature* 55.4 (Winter 2009), 547–71.

J. D. McClatchy, 'Elizabeth Bishop: Some Notes on "One Art"', in *White Paper: On Contemporary American Poetry* (Columbia University Press, 1989), 139–45.

Vidyan Ravinthiran, '"Manuelzinho", Brazil and Identity Politics', in Jonathan Ellis (ed.), *Reading Elizabeth Bishop: An Edinburgh Companion* (Edinburgh University Press, 2019), 33–47.

Chapter 6: Late travel poems

Elizabeth Bishop, 'A New Capital, Aldous Huxley, and Some Indians', *LOA*, 365–401.

Elizabeth Bishop, 'A Trip to Vigia', *LOA*, 461–8.

Kim Fortuny, *Elizabeth Bishop: The Art of Travel* (University Press of Colorado, 2003).

Jeffrey Gray, *Mastery's End: Travel and Postwar American Poetry* (University of Georgia Press, 2005).

Vidyan Ravinthiran, *Elizabeth Bishop's Prosaic* (Bucknell University Press, 2015), 179–98 ('"Santarém" and the Aesthetic Claim').

Ellen Bryant Voigt, 'A Varied Pulse', in *The Art of Syntax* (Graywolf Press, 2009), 79–97. ('The Moose').

Charles Wagley, *Amazon Town: A Study of Man in the Tropics* (1953; rpt Alfred A. Knopf, 1964).

Neil L. Whitehead, 'South America /Amazonia: The Forest of Marvels', in Peter Hulme and Tim Youngs (eds), *The Cambridge Companion to Travel Writing* (Cambridge University Press, 2002), 122–38.

Publisher's acknowledgements

Index

For the benefit of digital users, indexed terms that span two pages (e.g., 52–53) may, on occasion, appear on only one of those pages.

WRITING AND SCRIPT
A Very Short Introduction
Andrew Robinson

Without writing, there would be no records, no history, no books, and no emails. Writing is an integral and essential part of our lives; but when did it start? Why do we all write differently and how did writing develop into what we use today? All of these questions are answered in this *Very Short Introduction*. Starting with the origins of writing five thousand years ago, with cuneiform and Egyptian hieroglyphs, Andrew Robinson explains how these early forms of writing developed into hundreds of scripts including the Roman alphabet and the Chinese characters.

'User-friendly survey.'

Steven Poole, The Guardian

www.oup.com/vsi

BESTSELLERS
A Very Short Introduction
John Sutherland

'I rejoice', said Doctor Johnson, 'to concur with the Common Reader.' For the last century, the tastes and preferences of the common reader have been reflected in the American and British bestseller lists, and this *Very Short Introduction* takes an engaging look through the lists to reveal what we have been reading - and why. John Sutherland shows that bestseller lists monitor one of the strongest pulses in modern literature and are therefore worthy of serious study. Along the way, he lifts the lid on the bestseller industry, examines what makes a book into a bestseller, and asks what separates bestsellers from canonical fiction.

'His amiable trawl through the history of popular books is frequently entertaining'

Scott Pack, The Times

ENGLISH LITERATURE
A Very Short Introduction
Jonathan Bate

Sweeping across two millennia and every literary genre, acclaimed scholar and biographer Jonathan Bate provides a dazzling introduction to English Literature. The focus is wide, shifting from the birth of the novel and the brilliance of English comedy to the deep Englishness of landscape poetry and the ethnic diversity of Britain's Nobel literature laureates. It goes on to provide a more in-depth analysis, with close readings from an extraordinary scene in King Lear to a war poem by Carol Ann Duffy, and a series of striking examples of how literary texts change as they are transmitted from writer to reader.

{No reviews}

FRENCH LITERATURE
A Very Short Introduction
John D. Lyons

The heritage of literature in the French language is rich, varied, and extensive in time and space; appealing both to its immediate public, readers of French, and also to aglobal audience reached through translations and film adaptations. *French Literature: A Very Short Introduction* introduces this lively literary world by focusing on texts - epics, novels, plays, poems, and screenplays - that concern protagonists whose adventures and conflicts reveal shifts in literary and social practices. From the hero of the medieval *Song of Roland* to the Caribbean heroines of *Tituba, Black Witch of Salem* or the European expatriate in Japan in *Fear and Trembling*, these problematic protagonists allow us to understand what interests writers and readers across the wide world of French.

www.oup.com/vsi

GERMAN LITERATURE
A Very Short Introduction
Nicholas Boyle

German writers, from Luther and Goethe to Heine, Brecht, and Günter Grass, have had a profound influence on the modern world. This *Very Short Introduction* presents an engrossing tour of the course of German literature from the late Middle Ages to the present, focussing especially on the last 250 years. Emphasizing the economic and religious context of many masterpieces of German literature, it highlights how they can be interpreted as responses to social and political changes within an often violent and tragic history. The result is a new and clear perspective which illuminates the power of German literature and the German intellectual tradition, and its impact on the wider cultural world.

'Boyle has a sure touch and an obvious authority...this is a balanced and lively introduction to German literature.'

Ben Hutchinson, TLS

THE GREAT
DEPRESSION AND
NEW DEAL
A Very Short Introduction
Rich Rauchway

The book examines a key sampling of New Deal programs, ranging from the National Recovery Agency and the Securities and Exchange Commission, to the Public Works Administration and Social Security, revealing why some worked and others did not. In the end, Rauchway concludes, it was the coming of World War II that finally generated the political will to spend the massive amounts of public money needed to put Americans back to work. And only the Cold War saw the full implementation of New Deal policies abroad--including the United Nations, the World Bank, and the International Monetary Fund.

www.oup.com/vsi